YOU AND YOUR CHURCH

An In-depth Review of the Church of God
Cleveland, Tennessee

Michael L. Baker

Michael L. Baker

2 Peter 1:10

CHURCH OF GOD INTERNATIONAL OFFICES
CLEVELAND, TENNESSEE

YOU AND YOUR CHURCH

ISBN: 978-1-59684-767-5

Copyright © 2013 by Church of God
Printed by Pathway Press
Cleveland, TN 37311
All Rights Reserved

TABLE OF CONTENTS

FOREWORD 7
ACKNOWLEDGEMENTS 9

PART ONE

A CHURCH FOR THE TWENTY-FIRST CENTURY 13
A Global Movement 15
YOU—The Greatest Resource 17
What Is the Church of God? 18
Local Church 21
Ministers and Laity 21
Statements of Faith 22
Church Membership 24
Church of God Statistics, 2012 29
Purpose—*You and Your Church* 36

PART TWO

THE INVESTMENT OF MONEY 39
Principle of Stewardship 39
Financial System (Nonprofit) 40
Local Structure 40
State or Regional Structure 47
International Structure 50
Ministers Retirement Plan 57
Accountability 57
Commitment 58

PART THREE

THE IMPORTANCE OF MANAGEMENT 61
A Call for Leadership 61
Management Model 62
International General Assembly 63
Local Structure 64
Affiliation with the Church of God—Associate Church 70
District Structure 71
State or Regional Structure 73
International Structure 80
Credentialed Ministers 95
Affiliations 97
The Importance of Management 97

PART FOUR

THE IMPERATIVE OF MISSION AND VISION 99

The Challenge.. 99
Mission 101
Priority Statements 103
Vision.. 104
Ministry Essentials 107
A Compelling Call for Change 109
Strategic Direction... 110
Mission and Vision Initiatives 111
The Imperative... 116

APPENDICES.. 119

Appendix A: Doctrinal Commitments............................ 119
Appendix B: Practical Commitments.............................. 121

INDEX 131
CONTACTS 133

CHARTS

Church of God Membership Survey,
    1962-2012 27
Church of God Statistics, 2012................. 29
Church of God Local Structure 69
Church of God District Structure............. 72
Church of God State Structure................. 79
Church of God Divisional Structure......... 85
International Executive Committee.......... 86
General Overseer 87
Assistant General Overseers and
    Secretary General 88
World Missions.. 94

GRAPHS

Membership Survey 28
Percentage of Churches by Attendance,
    2012 33
Churches and Memberships,
    USA, 2013... 34
World Missions Membership
    by Continent, 2013 35
Church of God Percentage of the
    Budgeted Tithe Distribution, 2012 53
The Investment of the Missions Dollar,
    2012 55
Churches and Credentialed Ministers
    Worldwide, 1962-2012........................... 96

FOREWORD

Since its birth more than a century ago, the Church of God has been a Pentecostal movement with a mission to reach the world for Jesus Christ. Where is God leading the church today? He is directing the Church of God as a global movement prepared to meet the demands and challenges for future ministry.

Every member and adherent of the Church of God needs to fully understand the tenets and operation of the church they support and serve. As members and leaders of the Church of God, we should know who we are, what we believe, and how we can effectively carry out the call and commission of Christ. As the church faces the dimensions of the twenty-first century, a clear focus must be upon its greatest resource—you.

You and Your Church presents an in-depth review describing what it means to be part of the Church of God. It is designed to serve as an informational resource and program of instruction for new membership classes, leadership development, study/cell groups, discipleship training and conferences, and individual review and study. Part One describes the Church of God as a church for the twenty-first century. Part Two reviews the financial system at all levels of the church. Part Three describes the management functions at all levels of the church, and Part Four affirms the imperative of the church's mission and vision.

Special thanks and appreciation is expressed to Dr. Michael L. Baker, author of *You and Your Church—2nd Revised Edition*, for his keen insights and commitment to the Church of God. Appreciation is presented to the Department of Business and Records for preparation of the statistical data and to the divisions for their assistance in gathering information representing the various ministry areas of the church.

The Church of God must be a driving force of Pentecostal witness united in one accord. What will it take? It will take *you and your church*—together!

Church of God
General Executive Committee

ACKNOWLEDGEMENTS

Making disciples is at the very heart of God. Adult Discipleship Co-ordinators, David and Lorna Gosnell, believe that part of the discipleship process is being aware of the church and its doctrine. *You and Your Church*, written by Michael L. Baker, is a wonderful tool for helping people to know their church.

As in any undertaking of this magnitude, there are countless people who deserve special thanks.

This project could not have been completed without Dr. Michael L. Baker taking precious time from his schedule as administrative bishop of North Georgia. Dr. Baker, it is with gratitude that we thank you for helping to make sure that *You and Your Church* was thoroughly updated to where our church is today. Words cannot adequately express our gratitude.

When David and I approached Dr. Mark L. Williams, general overseer for the Church of God, concerning the *You and Your Church* project update, the number one expression was that it would be a helpful tool for the local pastor. He stated that when serving as pastor, the *You and Your Church* materials were vital in his new membership classes. He further said that he was very much behind the project and was excited that this tool for the pastor was being updated.

Along with the support of Dr. Mark L. Williams, the entire Executive Committee, David M. Griffis, J. David Stephens, Wallace J. Sibley, and M. Thomas Propes have been strong supporters for the project's completion. We appreciate your support so much.

There is much church data that has been included in the pages of *You and Your Church*. Julian B. Robinson has been very instrumental in making sure we had access to the information that was required for this project. We are indebted to you for your help, Julian. Thank you!

Several other key people had a role in seeing this project to completion. Sharon Baker, the wife of the author, spent countless hours pouring over the pages in the editing process. Sharon, thank you! Lonzo Kirkland is responsible for the eye-catching design, and we are grateful to Lonzo for his creative work. Michael McDonald was tapped for design layout of the book. Design layout is very tedious work and requires someone who is meticulous. So, thank you, Michael, for making sure the text of the book was designed in a way to be easy on the eye to read. Pathway Press has printed the project for us by being competitive in pricing so that we could use our own publishing house to print it. Thank you, Terry L. Hart, and the Pathway Press team for helping us. When we asked around for the person we should get to copy edit our project, everyone said, "Nellie Keasling." Nellie, thank you for making sure that every grammatical rule was followed so that we could present this project in excellence! Last, but certainly not least, was Lenae Simmons, Men's Discipleship assistant. There are many processes that a project like this goes through before it is completed. Lenae made sure that all the pieces came together from all the people who played a part. Thank you, Lenae.

We pray that as the local church body begins to pour through the pages of *You and Your Church* that you will understand what a wonderful, dynamic church you are associated with—a church that you can be proud to say is, "my church." We also pray that this will be another milestone tool that moves you closer to Christ in your discipleship walk.

David H. and Lorna V. Gosnell
Adult Discipleship Coordinators

PART ONE

A CHURCH FOR THE TWENTY-FIRST CENTURY

While the twentieth century was dramatic for the Church of God, one of the realities of the emerging twenty-first century is that yesterday's victories are no guarantee of tomorrow's success. The world is experiencing enormous changes—changes that are occurring so rapidly that they are difficult to understand, evaluate, or determine how to appropriately respond. However, in the midst of change is the challenge to perpetually look through the lens of tomorrow and catch a glimpse of the opportunities available for ministry in the future.

Envisioning the role of the Church of God as a relevant movement, it is imperative that the church . . .

- Appropriate God's Word as the criterion for all church ministries and personal living.

- Reach the whole world with the gospel of Jesus Christ.

- Develop ministers for maximum efficiency in declaring the gospel and strengthening local churches.

- Nurture believers in spiritual growth and personal development.

- Encourage lay witnessing and ministry participation in all believers.

- Establish believers as stewards of God's provisions in keeping with Biblical principles.

- Implement the expansion and outreach of local congregations in ministry to contemporary needs.

- Plant life-giving churches in the fulfillment of the Great Commission.

- Challenge families to live by the authority of God's Word and to implement its values into everyday living.

- Promote and build Scriptural leadership models at every level of church structure.

As the Church of God confronts the complex changes of an emerging future, we must be prepared to face transitions and meet the challenges of the present and future generations.

Confronting the challenges, the Church of God must . . .

- Affirm the inerrancy, power, and authority of God's Word.

- Emphasize the supremacy and strength daily prayer provides believers seeking God's divine guidance.

- Encourage awareness of the revival dynamics occurring throughout the world.

- Prepare for a first-century revival in order to fulfill the Great Commission.

- Focus upon the continual development and implementation of a ministry strategy for the Church of God.

- Build on our strengths and explore the spiritual resources necessary for effective local church ministry.

- Commit to the priorities of training and equipping leaders, making disciples, and affirming believers for a Pentecostal witness.

- Seek a fresh anointing of the Holy Spirit to face the challenges before us.

Our message is immutable. However, we must utilize all available methods and resources to share the life-changing power of Jesus Christ. The mission of the church is to "go into all the world" (Mark 16:15) and "make disciples" (Matthew 28:19). While our message and mission are constant, our approach and techniques of ministry must be flexible to meet the demands of the future. Our purpose is to be a *relevant church for the twenty-first century!*

A GLOBAL MOVEMENT

Since its beginning, the Church of God has been a "movement"—a moving church that is activated by the Holy Spirit. It is not just a regional or national movement, but a global movement with a mission of ministry to all humanity. It was birthed as a movement and has remained so for more than 125 years.

The Church of God had its humble beginning in a crude meeting house about two miles from the Tennessee-North Carolina boundary in 1886. A small group of sincere Christians had a deep desire for a closer relationship and life with Christ. They were eager for spiritual renewal and possessed an entrenched conviction to seek God for His power, guidance, and presence. They embraced the process of moving. They were on a mission.

Realizing the futility of reforming their churches, they established a new church whose objective would be to restore sound Scriptural doctrines of the Bible, encourage deeper consecration, and promote evangelism and Christian service. The beginning was small. Upon invitation, eight people stepped forward to establish this infant church called the Christian Union. Twenty-one years later, its name was changed to Church of God.

From this seemingly small, insignificant origin, it has grown to be an influential, worldwide, Pentecostal denomination with International Offices located in Cleveland, Tennessee. With more than 7 million recorded members in almost 180 countries and territories, the Church of God is comprised of approximately 37,000 local congregations and more than 38,000 ministers globally. The cover article of TIME magazine for April 5, 1993, titled, "The Church Search," reported the status of changing church denominations in America. Richard N. Ostling, the writer, described the rate of loss and gain in church membership between 1965 and 1989. The graphic showed the Church of God (Cleveland, Tennessee) with the largest percentage of growth (183%) in America during the reported time period. By comparison with a 1993 article, the statistical survey of 1962–2012 demonstrates a 484 percent membership growth in the USA/Canada and a 1,782 percent growth rate in worldwide membership.

In *Spiritual Balance: Reclaiming the Promise*, Dr. R. Lamar Vest provides a number of essentials that describe the marks of a true movement. A synopsis of these descriptors is listed below:

- A movement is person-centered rather than structure-centered. A movement gives priority to the needs of people.

- Movements are led by visionaries who are actively involved in the mission and work of the movement.

- A movement concentrates on call and mission.

- A movement views human resources as its greatest capital.

- A religious movement determines direction and makes decisions based on divine authority. A true movement never becomes a slave to programs and finances but follows the leadership of the Holy Spirit.

- Movements are dynamic, in a constant state of "going" forward.

Throughout its history, the Church of God has been a distinctive movement focused upon communicating the gospel in the power of the Holy Spirit. The call is still clear today. It is a call for world evangelization. It is a call to discipleship and prayer. It is a call of commitment. It is a call for the Church of God to be a channel for Pentecostal witness to all people around the world. If we are to continue as a twenty-first century Pentecostal movement, we must be Spirit-filled and Spirit-directed believers who possess a passion for missional ministry. That's our calling!

YOU—THE GREATEST RESOURCE

The vitality of any movement arises from its sense of identity. As members of the Church of God, we should know who we are, what we believe, and how we can effectively carry out the call and commission of Christ.

All members of the Church of God need to fully understand the tenets and operation of the church that they support and serve. As the church faces dimensions of the twenty-first century, a clear focus must be upon its greatest resource—you.

- *You*—the faces of millions around the world who have committed to the cause of Christ and the Church of God.

- *You*—the multitude of disciples who have accepted the commandment of the Great Commission.

- *You*—the thousands of ministers who have heard the call of God and have affirmed the role of servant leadership.

- *You*—every member and adherent who steps forward and joins the battalion of believers sharing the "good news" with the world.

The designation "the body" is used to refer to the physical body of Christ that He gave on Calvary. The body is also a reference to a local church. The word church (Greek, *ekklesia*) is defined as a group of "called-out ones."

The church is an assembly of professing believers. It is an assembly of those who have their faith in Jesus Christ (Romans 10:9), as an outward evidence to an inward reality of having their sins forgiven. Philippians 2:15, 16 says, "You shine like stars in the universe as you hold out the word of life." The church is a corporate light of hope shining in a world of darkness.

The Scriptures present Christ as the head of the body, which is the Church. The members of His body are to "grow up into him who is the Head, that is, Christ" (Ephesians 4:15). Every Christian is called to do the work of ministry and to build up the body of Christ. The goal of the church is to equip, minister to, and build up every believer toward the achievement of spiritual maturity. The church grows spiritually and numerically when each part of the body—each you of the church—lives under the control of Christ. Each you of the Church of God has been called out—called out by Christ to "shine like stars in the universe."

The greatest resource of the church is you. Every local congregation is formed when believers are joined together into one unified body. If the Church of God is to be a growing and healthy twenty-first century church, then it must recognize, train, support, and mobilize its greatest resource—you.

WHAT IS THE CHURCH OF GOD?

The Church of God was founded in 1886 upon the principles of Christ as they are revealed in the Bible—the Word of God. It has its foundation of faith and practice in the Scriptures, and the daily life experiences of its constituents are scripturally focused.

The Church of God is . . .

- **Christian**

    First and foremost, the Church of God is a determinedly Christian church. It is built upon the person of Jesus Christ, the Son of God. The doctrines and practices of the church are based upon His teachings.

- **Protestant**

     The Church of God is founded upon the principles of Protestant-ism, although it is not a traditional follower of any specific leader of the Protestant Reformation. The denomination stands firmly for justi-fication by faith, the priesthood of believers, the authority of the Bi-ble, religious freedom, and the separation of church and state. It stands against abuses and extravagances of ecclesiastical ritualism and dogmatism.

- **Foundational**

     The Church of God subscribes to the following five foundational Christian doctrines:

     1. The inerrancy and infallibility of the Bible
     2. The Virgin Birth and complete deity of Christ
     3. The atoning sacrifice of Christ's death for the sins of the world
     4. The literal resurrection of the body
     5. Christ's second coming in bodily form to earth.

- **Evangelical**

     Evangelical is the term used to describe those who affirm the primary doctrines revealed in the Scriptures. These doctrines include the inspiration and authority of the Word of God, the Trinity, the deity and virgin birth of Jesus Christ, salvation by faith in the atoning death of Christ, His bodily resurrection and ascension to the right hand of the Father, the ministry of the Holy Spirit, the second coming of Christ, and the spiritual unity of believers in Jesus Christ.

     The Church of God has aligned itself with the basic statement of faith of the National Association of Evangelicals (NAE), the largest association of Evangelicals in the USA. Members of NAE subscribe to a common statement of faith. To this extent, the Church of God can be described as positioned in the mainstream of Evangelical Protestantism.

- **Pentecostal**

    In 1896, many members of the Church of God experienced a spiritual outpouring they identified as the baptism of the Holy Spirit. Because it was so similar to the experience of the early Christians on the Day of Pentecost, it came to be called a Pentecostal experience, an enrichment of the Christian life through the power of the Holy Spirit that empowered believers to be effective witnesses of Christ. The principal distinctive of the Church of God as a Pentecostal organization is its belief in speaking with other tongues as the Spirit gives the utterance and that this is the initial evidence of the baptism in the Holy Spirit.

- **Charismatic**

    The gifts of the Spirit (Greek, *charismata*) appeared early in the life and ministry of the Church of God. The gifts can be divided into three categories: (1) the gifts of revelation, (2) the gifts of power, and (3) the gifts of utterance or inspiration. First, the gifts of revelation are the word of wisdom, the word of knowledge, and the discerning of spirits. Second, the gifts of power are faith, miracles, and gifts of healing. Third, the gifts of utterance and inspiration are prophecy, tongues, and interpretation. The Holy Spirit bestows these gifts, and those who accept the validity of these gifts are called charismatic.

- **Evangelistic**

    From its inception, the Church of God has been a revival movement. Evangelism has been in the forefront of all its activities. The church has maintained an aggressive effort to take the message of Christ throughout the world by all means and methods. Every program of the church reflects an evangelistic attitude: revivalism, conferences, worship services, teaching, preaching, and missionary efforts.

- **Organized**

    The magnitude of the Great Commission requires a united effort. This united endeavor is efficiently served by guidance, support, resources, and leadership from a common center. The Church of God is centrally organized, which helps facilitate the fulfillment of the mission of the church. Centralized church government has administration from the international, state, or regional, and local levels.

The control and governance of the Church of God rests with the laity and ministers, who jointly form a governing body called the International General Assembly. Benefits of a centralized government include the following: uniformity of doctrine and practice; principles that bind together local churches; membership commitments in all churches; expansion and extension of fellowship; accountability; cooperative decision-making; and united efforts in evangelism and world outreach.

LOCAL CHURCH

Within the Church of God, the local church is recognized as the foundation of all ministry activities and is committed to acknowledge, affirm, strengthen, and support the central importance of the ministry of every local congregation. This is accomplished through proclamation of the joy and power of worship; clear understanding of spiritual gifts and their operation in the church; care in appointment of pastors, with emphasis on compatibility and interrelationships between congregation and leaders; strengthening the pastoral role as spiritual shepherd; emphasis on training laity for effective ministry; and development of methods for objective evaluation of local church ministries.

MINISTERS AND LAITY

It is the belief of the Church of God that from within the priesthood of all believers, God specifically selects, calls, anoints, and commissions individuals for extraordinary service and leadership. This special calling is of God's sovereign will, characterized by individuals with spiritual passion, love for the lost, total involvement, lifelong sacrifice, servant leadership, and commitment as a credentialed minister.

Ministers in the Church of God are ranked as ordained bishop, ordained minister, exhorter, minister of music, and minister of Christian education. They achieve these levels of ministry through a profession of faith, commitment to the church, training, internship, ministerial experience, and fulfillment of credential requirements.

Ministers and laity are partners in ministry in every area of the church. Church of God polity encourages laity to assume a rightful Biblical role as full partners in ministry throughout every area of the church. This is realized through commitment to train, inspire, equip, and release laity for ministry in strategic areas of the local church and community service; development of lay leaders; and joint interaction between lay and ministerial leadership in establishing harvest goals and objectives for the Church of God.

STATEMENTS OF FAITH

The Holy Scriptures are recognized as the true source of Church of God faith. The Church of God believes the whole Bible to be completely and equally inspired and that it is the written Word of God. The Declaration of Faith is the official expression of Church of God doctrine.

DECLARATION OF FAITH

WE BELIEVE:
1. In the verbal inspiration of the Bible.

2. In one God eternally existing in three persons; namely, the Father, Son, and Holy Ghost.

3. That Jesus Christ is the only begotten Son of the Father, conceived of the Holy Ghost, and born of the Virgin Mary. That Jesus was crucified, buried, and raised from the dead. That he ascended to heaven and is today at the right hand of the Father as the Intercessor.

4. That all have sinned and come short of the glory of God and that repentance is commanded of God for all and necessary for forgiveness of sins.

5. That justification, regeneration, and the new birth are wrought by faith in the blood of Jesus Christ.

6. In sanctification subsequent to the new birth, through faith in the blood of Christ; through the Word, and by the Holy Ghost.

7. Holiness to be God's standard of living for His people.

8. In the baptism with the Holy Ghost subsequent to a clean heart.

9. In speaking with other tongues as the Spirit gives utterance and that it is the initial evidence of the baptism in the Holy Ghost.

10. In water baptism by immersion, and all who repent should be baptized in the name of the Father, and of the Son, and of the Holy Ghost.

11. Divine healing is provided for all in the atonement.

12. In the Lord's Supper and washing of the saints' feet.

13. In the premillennial second coming of Jesus. First, to resurrect the righteous dead and to catch away the living saints to Him in the air. Second, to reign on the earth a thousand years.

14. In the bodily resurrection; eternal life for the righteous, and eternal punishment for the wicked.

DOCTRINAL AND PRACTICAL COMMITMENTS

The Church of God has its foundation of theological and practical commitments rooted in the Scriptures. Since the inception of the church, the basic doctrines have remained constant. However, throughout its history, the church has periodically amplified its practical beliefs according to how our Statements of Faith affect us in light of today's globally diversified cultures.

The New Testament is accepted as the only standard for government and discipline. The Old Testament is fundamental to Church of God faith and practice as it is interpreted and fulfilled by the New Testament. According to the *General Assembly Minutes*,

> The Church of God stands now, as it has always stood, for the whole Bible rightly divided, and for the New Testament as the only rule for government and discipline. It has been necessary at times for the International General Assembly of the church to search the Scriptures and interpret the meaning of the Bible to arrive at what is the true and proper teaching of the church on various subjects, but always with the purpose and intention to base our teachings strictly upon the Bible (74th A., 2012, p. 22).

A complete listing of Doctrinal Commitments is provided in Appendix A. Appendix B provides a full description of the Practical Commitments. A study of the Statements of Faith, along with Scriptural references, reveals the commitment of the Church of God to Biblical integrity and serves as a basis for Christian living and practice.

CHURCH MEMBERSHIP

Membership in the Church of God calls for a public commitment and identity with the church. New believers are assimilated into the life of the congregation. Inclusion of new members in the Church of God has been evidenced throughout its history. The success of evangelism outreach, planting of new churches, and world evangelization has demonstrated outstanding growth.

Church membership should be conceptualized, not as a destination, but rather as a doorway that leads to discipleship and involvement in ministry. A fresh paradigm calls for the church to identify, enlist, nurture, disciple, train, place, and support resource teams of lay leaders—members of the church—who will implement new ministries to meet the needs of all age groups.

Procedurally, individuals presenting themselves for membership should be fully informed of the doctrine, teachings, government, and heritage of the Church of God. Upon the completion of the informational steps, the pastor leads prospective members in the following charge and Covenant of Membership.

COVENANT OF MEMBERSHIP

- You realize in presenting yourself for membership that you are assuming a solemn obligation, and it is expected that you will always be true to your promise and faithfully fulfill and discharge your obligation as a loyal member.

- Do you publicly confess and testify that you know the Lord Jesus Christ as your personal Savior in the full pardon of your sins? [The applicant will answer, I do.]

- Are you willing to walk in the light of the Scripture as it shines upon your path? [I am.]

- Are you willing to abide by and subscribe to the discipline of the Church of God as outlined by the Scripture and set forth in the Minutes of the General Assembly? [I am.]

- Are you willing to support the Church with your attendance and temporal means to the best of your ability as the Lord prospers you? [I am.]

- Do you agree to be subject to the counsel and admonition of those who are over you in the Lord? [I do.]

- If there be any member who has a legal objection to any of these becoming members of the Church, the objector may now so state.

- By the authority vested in me as a minister of the Church of God, I take great pleasure in welcoming you into this membership and extending to you the right hand of fellowship. May I encourage you to call for the services of your pastor when needed.

- I have confidence that you will ever be a faithful member and a blessing to the Church and that the Church will be a blessing to you. I pray our fellowship will always be bound together with unbroken love.

CHURCH OF GOD MEMBERSHIP SURVEY, 1962–2012

A survey of membership statistics for 1962–2012 reveals substantial increases during the fifty-year period.

CHURCH OF GOD
MEMBERSHIP SURVEY, 1962–2012

GEN. ASSEMBLY	USA/CANADA	WORLD	TOTAL
1962	190,776	178,019	368,795
1964	206,141	190,086	396,227
1966	221,156	228,363	449,519
1968	244,261	266,773	511,034
1970	263,388	272,848	536,236
1972	292,833	342,499	635,332
1974	325,727	404,184	729,911
1976	359,632	469,011	828,643
1978	388,670	576,768	965,438
1980	430,308	868,709	1,299,017
1982	470,000	917,132	1,387,132
1984	504,731	969,359	1,474,090
1986	546,728	1,105,361	1,652,089
1988	587,495	1,225,509	1,813,004
1990	626,108	1,511,747	2,137,855
1992	677,888	2,041,892	2,719,780
1994	721,476	2,924,933	3,646,409
1996	782,729	3,316,000	4,098,729
1998	862,932	4,150,000	5,012,932
2000	897,835	4,868,845	5,766,680
2002	950,364	5,552,426	6,502,790
2004	995,363	5,798,753	6,794,116
2006	1,039,925	5,842,474	6,882,399
2008	1,081,165	5,822,804	6,903,971
2010	1,084,414	5,701,606	6,786,020
2012	1,114,786	5,827,799	6,942,585

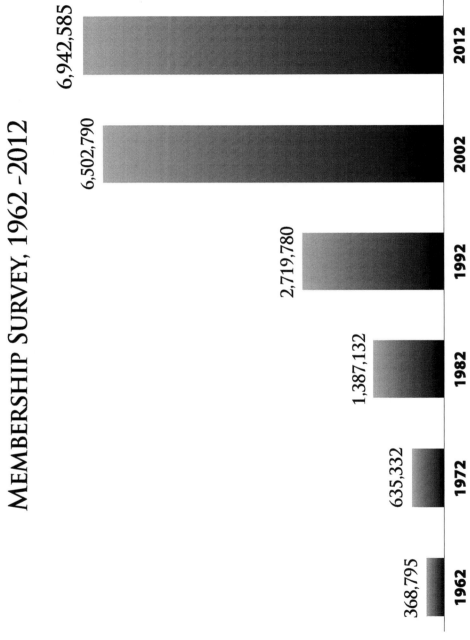

MEMBERSHIP SURVEY, 1962 –2012

Year	Membership
1962	368,795
1972	635,332
1982	1,387,132
1992	2,719,780
2002	6,502,790
2012	6,942,585

A review of average net membership growth rate for the two-year terms from 1962–2012 shows an average increase per term of 7.6 percent in the USA/Canada and 15.6 percent throughout the rest of the world. Total percentage growth statistics for the fifty-year period demonstrates a growth rate in membership of 484 percent in the USA/Canada, an astounding 3,173 percent for World Missions, and 1,782 percent for the total church worldwide.

TOTAL PERCENTAGE GROWTH RATE, 1962–2012

USA/CANADA	484%
WORLD	3,173%
TOTAL CHURCH	1,782%

CHURCH OF GOD STATISTICS, 2012

The following statistics provide a ministry review of the Church of God:

CHURCHES:

USA/Canada	6,567
World Missions	30,513
TOTAL	**37,080**

CHURCH MEMBERSHIP:

USA/Canada	1,114,786
World Missions	5,827,799
TOTAL	**6,942,585**

MINISTERS:

Ordained Bishops	11,705
Ordained Ministers	9,772
Exhorters	16,179
Minister of Music/Christian Education	363
TOTAL	**38,019**

GENERAL MINISTRIES

Communications
  Internet Ministry
    Unique Visitors   59,000
    Page Views   245,000
    Site Visits   71,000

  Faith News Network
    Subscribers   11,000
  Emails Sent Each Month   250,000

DIVISIONS AND MINISTRIES

DIVISION OF CARE MINISTRIES

Chaplains Commission (Vocational Chaplains)
  Military Chaplains
    Active Duty   56
    Reserve   16
    Civil Air Patrol   2
  Institutional Chaplains
    Clinical   80
    Veterans Affairs   8
    Correctional   27
    University Campus   3
    Counselor/Pastoral   11
    Industry   17
    International   34
  Volunteer (Community Service Chaplains)   10,000
Benevolence
  Home for Children   3
  Youth Ranches   2
  International Programs   2
  Widows Care Center   1

DIVISION OF EDUCATION MINISTRIES

Postsecondary Educational Institutions

Countries Represented	68
Graduate Degree-Granting Institutions Worldwide	13
Degree-Granting Institutions Worldwide	22
Bible Institutes and Christian Service Schools Worldwide	78
Students Worldwide (Residential and Extension)	35,000

Ministerial Development (Participants/Candidates)

Lay Leadership Development	772
Calling And Ministries Studies (CAMS)	436
Ministerial Internship Program (MIP)	431
Certificate In Ministerial Studies (CIMS)	2,934
Exhorter Ministerial Licensing Studies	290
Ordained Minister Licensing Studies	109
Ordained Bishop Licensing Studies	101

DIVISION OF WORLD EVANGELIZATION

USA Missions

Black Ministries	
Congregations of African Descent	654
Hispanic Ministries (USA)	
Congregations	925
Hispanic Bible Institutes	97
Enrollment Hispanic Ministerial Institutions	1,410
Ministry in Geographical States	21
Hispanic Regions	8
Ministry to the Military	
Christian Servicemen's Centers	35
Military Contact Churches	201

World Missions

Countries Served	177
Churches	30,370
Missions and Preaching Stations	4,273
Ministers	20,118
Members	5,834,718
Bible Schools	124
Bible School Enrollment	30,131
Missionaries:	
From the USA/Canada	263
From Other Countries	349
National Leaders	254
World Missions Giving, 2011–2012	$25,048,823
Men and Women of Action	4,800

DIVISION OF DISCIPLESHIP

Youth and Discipleship

Sunday Schools USA/Canada	5,021
Sunday School Weekly Attendance USA/Canada	386,617
Sunday Morning Average Worship Attendance USA/Canada	615,978
Chartered Young Ladies Ministries	2,301
Chartered Joy Belles	3,203
Chartered Bluebelles	3,205
Chartered Little Sweethearts	355
Counselor's Enrichment Training Course (CETC) Graduates	6,194

Men's Discipleship

LifeBuilders Men's Discipleship Chapters	2,132
Local Church Lay Coordinators	1,022
State Lay Boards	39

Women's Discipleship

Chartered Women's Discipleship Groups	4,588

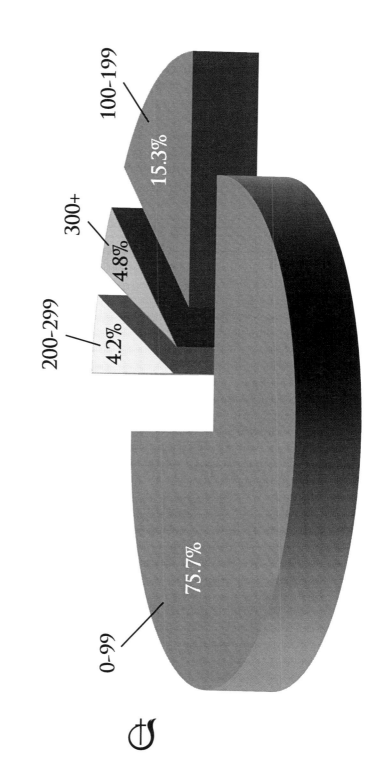

Percentage of Churches by Attendance, 2012
USA/Canada, Sunday Morning Worship

100-199 — 15.3%
300+ — 4.8%
200-299 — 4.2%
0-99 — 75.7%

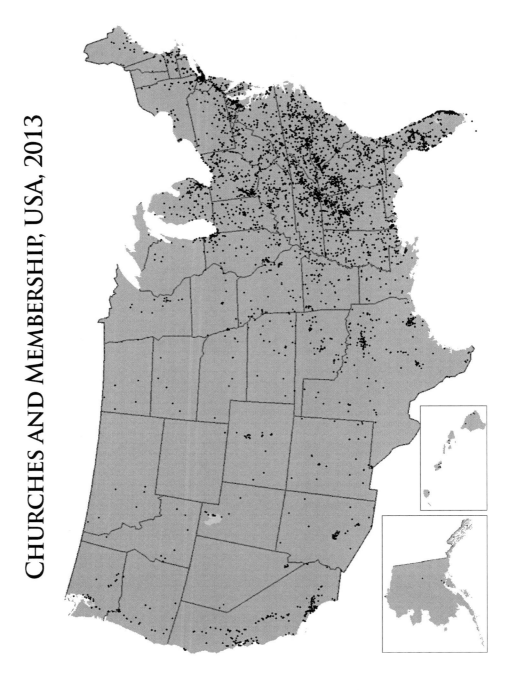

CHURCHES AND MEMBERSHIP, USA, 2013

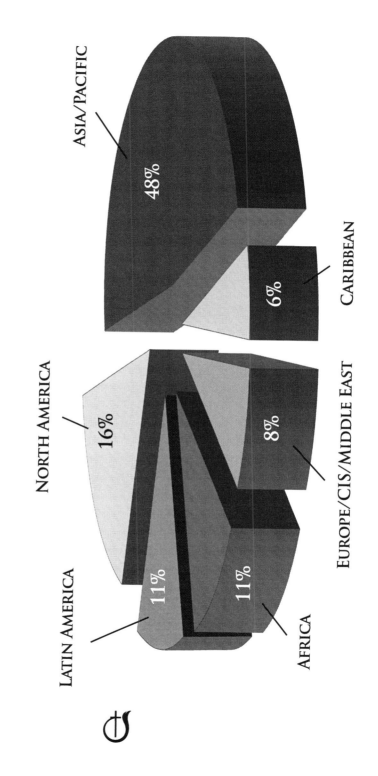

WORLD MISSIONS MEMBERSHIP
BY CONTINENT, 2013

ASIA/PACIFIC — 48%

CARIBBEAN — 6%

NORTH AMERICA — 16%

EUROPE/CIS/MIDDLE EAST — 8%

LATIN AMERICA — 11%

AFRICA — 11%

PURPOSE—YOU AND YOUR CHURCH

You and Your Church presents a concise ministry review for those who want to know what it means to be associated with the Church of God. This resource presents in four parts an overview of the Church of God, which includes the following:

- *Part One:*   *A Church For The Twenty-First Century*
- *Part Two:*   *The Investment Of Money*
- *Part Three:*   *The Importance Of Management*
- *Part Four:*   *The Imperative Of Mission And Vision*

This presentation is designed to inform Church of God members and adherents who are interested in learning more about the church, as well as individuals who may wish to unite in membership.

The materials include the following:
- Book, *You and Your Church—2nd Revised Edition*
- Instructor's Guide
- Informational Booklet, *You and Your Church*

Copies of the materials are available in singles or multiples from the Church of God Division of Discipleship at *www.youandyourchurch.com* (phone toll free: 888.766.9009, office: 423.478.7286) or Pathway Press, *www.pathwaybookstore.com* (phone toll free: 800.553.8506). Local churches may wish to maintain a supply of these resources as information for interested individuals and new members' classes. A combination of the book, *You and Your Church—2nd Revised Edition* and a copy of the general informational booklet can be used effectively as a resource for those wanting to know more about the Church of God.

You and Your Church is intended for use with the following methods:
- As a series for new membership classes
- Presentation as an adult elective in discipleship settings
- Leadership development

- Small study/cell group
- Individual review and study
- Available online for individual study and group interactive discussion at *www.youandyourchurch.com*, Church of God Division of Discipleship
- *You and Your Church* Discipleship Conferences

The presentation format and resources include the following:

- Class segments presented in 40-50-minute sessions by the local pastor or designated instructor for new membership class, adult electives in discipleship settings, small study groups, or individual study. Sessions may be in a classroom setting or live web-conferencing.

- *You and Your Church—2nd Revised Edition* book for each person attending the sessions.

- *You and Your Church—Instructor's Guide* to resource the instructor regarding exposition of content and method of presentation.

- A Church of God introductory booklet, *You and Your Church*, for each person attending the sessions and, in addition, use as a general informational tool for those who are interested in learning more about the Church of God.

- *You and Your Church* Discipleship Conference for the purpose of sharing discipleship initiatives, resources, and training in corporate settings.

PART TWO

THE INVESTMENT OF MONEY

PRINCIPLE OF STEWARDSHIP

The scope of Christian stewardship is multidimensional. Its boundaries have been expanded to include time, talents, service, possessions, and much more. A basic principle relating to the work of a committed steward is the focus upon the discriminating management of possessions. Scriptures present the practice of tithing and giving as a positive plan for a partnership with God.

The framework of tithing is the revelation of a divine plan. It is the Scriptural principle that one-tenth of one's income belongs to God, together with offerings above the tithe. Tithing and giving, when followed in a conscientious program of worship, provide adequate financing of God's work. Each contribution of tithe and offerings by every single individual, regardless of age or socioeconomic status, is an investment in the ministries of the church.

Part Two—The Investment of Money reviews the financial system used in the Church of God and chronicles the receipt and disbursement of contributions. This segment will examine at the local, state, and international levels the source of monies, the expenditures of funds, and the method of accountability.

When individuals make an investment, they expect a return. While the secular world understands this principle, Christians understand the spiritual significance. The spiritual focus in the practice of tithing and giving is upon people rather than money. The concentration of Christ's teachings on money reveals that personal regard for and uses of money are reflected in the character of the believer. The value a Christian places upon possessions, and what he does with them, exhibits the foundation of faith and a personal walk with Christ.

Although tithing is not a test of membership in the Church of God, it is a Biblical principle that promises blessings to the believer. Every faithful tithing member of the church should know the importance, value, and procedures for the receipt and distribution of funds in the church.

FINANCIAL SYSTEM (NONPROFIT)

According to the objectives and purposes for which the affairs of the Church of God are conducted, it is classified as a religious, nonprofit organization. Article II, Temporal Nature, of the Bylaws of the Church of God states: "The Church of God is incorporated in the state of Tennessee (U.S.A.) as a not-for-profit organization and is recognized as a 501 (c) (3) corporation under the Internal Revenue Code (U.S.A.) or the corresponding sections of any prior or future Internal Revenue Code (U.S.A.)." The operation of the denomination is not for financial gain or profit of any person or group. All net receipts of the church are to be used for religious, charitable, and educational purposes.

LOCAL STRUCTURE

The essence of the Church of God is the local congregation. The state/regional and international levels exist to promote, coordinate, resource, and emphasize the various ministries of the church. However, the Church of God recognizes the local church as the foundation of all ministry activities. The financial system of the church focuses upon centralized governance, with checks and balances at each level of operation.

TITHE AND OFFERINGS

According to the *Church of God General Assembly Minutes*:

The principle of local churches giving a tithe of their tithe for worldwide ministry has been a part of Church of God practice from its earliest days. As a Scriptural principle . . . and an approved program of the International General Assembly, tithing the tithe provides a way for each local church to have a part in contributing to the worldwide ministry of the church. Through faithfulness and consistency in this practice, the local church extends its ministry far beyond its own borders and releases God's blessing in the same way that a church member's practice of tithing brings blessings into his/her personal life (74th A., 2012, S43, III, A., p. 130).

The International General Assembly Minutes further states: "All members and ministers of the Church of God shall pay tithes into the church where they are members" (74th A., 2012, II, 1, p. 128). The financial base of the denomination is the tithe (10%) contributed by the individual members and adherents of the local church.

Above the tithe, local churches receive offerings for various ministry endeavors. Offerings may include giving in worship services, Sunday school classes, capital and building-fund programs, special ministry enterprises, and any other special project the local church may sponsor.

CHURCH TREASURER OR CHURCH ADMINISTRATOR

The local treasurer or church administrator is the financial and business representative of the congregation. He or she is appointed by the pastor and confirmed by the church council or the entire church body.

Qualifications
To serve as church treasurer one must be . . .

- A loyal member of the church, adhering to its teachings.

- Baptized in the Holy Spirit.

- Faithful in tithing.

- A regular church attender.

- One who performs duties under the supervision of the pastor and with his/her approval.

- One who works in harmony with the church's program and reflects a cooperative attitude with reference to the progress of the local church.

Duties and Responsibilities
The church treasurer shall . . .

- Determine and maintain accurate records of the church and other vital information pertaining to the local church.

- Keep accurate records of names and addresses of local church members.

- Record and maintain accurate minutes of all church conferences and business transactions.

- Maintain accurate records of all local church conferences and disbursements.

- Prepare monthly reports and send one copy to the secretary general and one copy to the state/regional overseer by the fifth (5th) of each month.

- Prepare financial reports for quarterly conferences.

- Provide a weekly itemized list of all receipts and disbursements for the pastor.

- Disburse money from the church treasury under the direction of the pastor.

FINANCE COMMITTEE

Each local church is encouraged to select a Finance Committee to assist in the management of local church funds. The Finance Committee normally consists of the church treasurer and two other members appointed by the pastor and confirmed by the Church and Pastor's Council and/or the members of the local church.

Qualifications
A member of the Finance Committee must be . . .

- A loyal member of the church, adhering to its teachings.

- Baptized in the Holy Spirit.

- Faithful in tithing.

- A regular church attender.

- One who works in harmony with the church's programs and reflects a cooperative attitude with reference to the progress of the local church.

Duties and Responsibilities
The Finance Committee shall . . .

1. Receive and count all monies.

2. Prepare funds for deposit.

Records and Reports

Each local church treasurer is required to send monthly reports, including the financial statement of tithes received, to the state/regional administrative bishop and the secretary general. The duties of the church treasurer include maintaining accurate records of all receipts and disbursements from the church treasury. In addition, the church treasurer prepares a financial report to be presented at regular church conferences consisting of the membership of the local church. The church conference also considers any other business that may be referred by the pastor and Church Council. All major disbursements of the local church should be approved by the membership of the local church in conference.

The entire local church budget is under the direct supervision of the pastor. All financial matters are reviewed by the church treasurer and Church Council, with recommendations and reports presented to the membership of the church in conference. The management of monies should be in keeping with the guidelines established by the International General Assembly of the Church of God and under the jurisdiction of the state/regional administrative bishop.

EXPENDITURES

The financial base of the local church consists of tithes, offerings, funding projects, and other enterprises. Primary expenditures are for administration, operational responsibilities, support of various local church ministries, and a tithe of tithe support to the state/regional and International Offices.

Administrative costs include providing for pastor's compensation and any other administrative staff. The basic compensation for pastors consists of the following:

- Salary designated according to the "Pastor's Minimum Compensation Scale" adopted by the International General Assembly.

- One-half of the pastor's Social Security tax.

- Health insurance coverage.

- Contribution by the local church to the Church of God Ministers' Retirement Plan of an amount equal to at least 5 percent of the salary compensation received by the pastor.

- Adequate housing accommodations and utilities.

This basic compensation is based upon availability of adequate tithe funds in the local church. Special considerations are provided for pastors where the tithe income is not sufficient to meet the minimum compensation requirements. Churches are encouraged to also provide other expenses necessary for the ministry and provide incentives based on increases in finance, pastoral responsibility, pastoral effectiveness, and longevity. Annually, the International Executive Council of the Church of God announces any cost-of-living adjustment in the pastor's compensation based on the U.S. government cost-of-living index.

Operational expenditures include those financial responsibilities necessary to maintain facilities and properties of the local church, such as mortgage, utilities, maintenance, and so forth.

Funds from the local church treasury also support various designated ministries. These may include missions, youth ministries, evangelism, music, outreach, benevolence, and many others.

As a function of the centralized government of the Church of God, each local congregation is required to do the following:

- Send the approved percentage of all tithes paid into the local treasury to the secretary general at the International Offices.

- Send an equal amount of the approved percentage to their state or regional treasurer with their monthly report.

This is called the "tithe of tithe," meaning each local church tithes ten percent (10%) of the total tithe received. The tithe of tithe provides the financial base of operation for both the state/regional and international levels of the Church of God.

Funds received from the local church are designated for the operation of ministry at the state or regional level, international level, evangelism support, and world missions.

Throughout its history, the Church of God has maintained a strong focus upon the principle of tithing. According to the *Church of God Book of Minutes* (Sixth, 1911), the Church of God encouraged tithes as God's plan of ministerial support. The church has maintained that tithing is a divine and perpetual system of church finance. In 1972, the International General Assembly affirmed a resolution on tithing which states the following:

TITHING

WHEREAS tithing is both a privilege of the individual and a part of God's plan for His people; and

WHEREAS tithing is clearly supported by both the Old and New Testaments as the basic plan of giving; and

WHEREAS the Church of God from its inception has preached and practiced tithing as a Scriptural injunction;

THEREFORE BE IT RESOLVED that the church urge its members to continued faithfulness and diligence in tithing;

BE IT FURTHER RESOLVED that all members be urged to place their tithe in the tithe fund of the local church for the expansion of its total ministries (54th A., 1972, p. 38).

At the 74th International General Assembly (2012), a resolution was adopted regarding Biblical Stewardship. Excerpts from the resolution state the following:

BIBLICAL STEWARDSHIP

BE IT RESOLVED THAT, pastors and local congregations be encouraged to teach and practice the principles of Biblical stewardship and that churches be encouraged to avail themselves of the latest available technology to enhance worship through tithing and offerings.

BE IT FURTHER RESOLVED THAT, we do hereby reaffirm our strong faith that our God "is able to do exceeding abundantly above all that we ask or think" (Ephesians 3:20), and that He "shall supply all your need according to his riches in glory by Christ Jesus" (Philippians 4:19) (74th A., 2012, p. 193).

For more than a century, the Church of God has been a giving church—a generous church. It is because of every "you" joining hearts and hands together, standing shoulder-to-shoulder in faithful stewardship that we have witnessed abundant ministry flourishing around the globe.

STATE OR REGIONAL STRUCTURE

Each local church is designated as part of an individual state or regional office in the USA and Canada. State or regional offices provide established boundaries, with designation of specific local churches under the jurisdiction of that office.

The administration of a Church of God state or regional office is under the supervision of the administrative bishop or sometimes called, state overseer. He, along with other state leaders, is responsible for the disbursements from the state treasury.

ADMINISTRATIVE BISHOP (STATE OVERSEER)

The administrative bishop is appointed by the International Executive Committee of the Church of God. A state or territorial administrative bishop can also be designated by the title of state/regional overseer. This individual must be a person of strong spiritual authority, and able to demonstrate capable leadership qualities. He is accountable to the International Executive Committee and to those whom he serves. According to the financial system of the Church of God, the administrative bishop is responsible for the oversight of the state budget.

Some specific financial duties include the following:

- Receive and maintain detailed records of all tithe-of-tithe contributions from local churches.

- Administrate the state or regional office budget.

- Maintain ministers' reports, church treasurers' reports, financial records, and other records of importance.

- Approve the selection, purchase, and construction of all church, parsonage, or properties, together with the respective district overseer.

- Receive the approval of the International Executive Committee before launching large financial state projects

- Make monthly reports to the general overseer.

STATE COUNCIL

The ministers of each state or region elect a board of councilors called the State Council. Along with the administrative bishop, the state council has the following financial responsibilities:

- Supervise the state missions fund, surplus tithes, state/regional properties, and all other funds received and disbursed by the state/regional treasury.

- Authorize the use of surplus tithe of tithes (i.e., remaining fund balance after normal budget expenditures are made) to supplement underpaid pastors and evangelists.

- Where funds are available, employ the state secretary and treasurer.

Many states with a substantial number of churches and membership employ a state secretary/treasurer who is responsible for the daily management of the state treasury under the direction of the administrative bishop and state council.

STATE BOARD OF TRUSTEES

In each state or region, the administrative bishop appoints a State Board of Trustees of not less than five members. Their responsibilities include making all necessary transactions or arrangements for the sale or transfer of property, or for the borrowing of money and pledging of property to secure the payment of the same, and to execute all necessary conveyances pursuant to the direction of the International Executive Committee.

RECEIPTS

The primary source of receipts for each state or regional office is the approved percentage of the tithe of tithe from every local church in the designated area. In addition, every state office may develop special projects as fund-raisers for various evangelism projects and ministry endeavors. Each state/regional department—evangelism, church planting, world missions, youth and discipleship, women's/men's ministries, laity, and so forth—may develop indigenous programs that provide sources of additional revenue.

EXPENDITURES

Primary expenditures are for administration of the state/regional office, operational responsibilities of the state facilities, appropriations supporting the various state departmental budgets, church planting, maintaining new field works, sustaining evangelism initiatives, and other special projects.

Administrative costs include providing for administrative bishop compensation and other administrative staff. The basic compensation for the administrative bishop and other administrative leaders includes a salary set by the International Executive Council, one-half Social Security tax, a minimum 5 percent of compensation for retirement plan, medical insurance, housing, and reimbursement of official ministry expenses incurred at the state/regional and general levels.

Operational expenditures include those financial responsibilities necessary to maintain state/regional facilities and properties such as offices, parsonages, campgrounds, camp facilities, and other state holdings.

Other major expenditures include appropriations for operation of the various state/regional departments. Each of the state/regional programs and projects are designed to serve as resources for local church ministries. All states and regions of the Church of God annually set specific goals for World Missions giving for world evangelization. Giving to World Missions is also a notable commitment of every local church.

INTERNATIONAL STRUCTURE

While local churches are part of a designated state or region, they are connected directly to the International Offices of the Church of God. Local church treasurers are required to submit local monthly reports, including a financial statement of tithes received and their contribution of the tithe of tithe to the secretary general.

The administration of the Church of God International Offices is under the supervision of the general overseer, three assistants, the secretary general, and 18 councilors who constitute the International Executive Council of the church. The International Executive Committee (general overseer, three assistants, and secretary general) is responsible for the day-to-day administration of the budget of the International Offices. The International Executive Council meets periodically during the year to conduct the business of the entire denomination between sessions of the International General Assembly.

INTERNATIONAL EXECUTIVE COUNCIL

Among the many duties and responsibilities of the International Executive Council, the following items pertain to money management:

- Consideration and action upon any and all matters pertaining to the general interest and welfare of the Church of God.

- Distribution of tithe of tithes sent to the International Offices from local churches.

- Annual approval of all divisional budgets. (A Budget Review Committee is appointed from the International Executive Council by the general overseer to review, discuss, and offer counsel and recommendations regarding divisional budgets.)

- Establishment of a loan fund to provide interim financing for churches in new fields.

GENERAL BOARD OF TRUSTEES

The General Board of Trustees consists of seven members, two who are designated as alternates, and are appointed at the International General Assembly by the International Executive Committee. Each appointee must be a member in good standing of the Church of God.

When the International General Assembly is not in session, the General Board of Trustees has power and authority to make all necessary transactions or arrangements for the sale or transfer of property, or for the borrowing of money and the pledging of real estate to secure the payment of the same, and to execute all necessary conveyances pursuant to the direction of the International Executive Committee. Any property (both real and personal) held by any of the boards of trustees (general, state, and local) is the property of the Church of God and shall be managed and controlled exclusively for the use and benefit of the Church of God.

RECEIPTS

As a function of the polity of the Church of God, each local church is required to send an approved percentage of all tithes paid monthly into the local treasury to the secretary general at the International Offices. These receipts are one of the primary sources of income at the international level.

Other major sources of revenue include contributions to World Missions, Benevolence Ministries, operation of Pathway Press (publishing ministry), educational institutions (tuition, etc.), church agencies, and various divisional and departmental programs.

Many divisions and their various departments of the International Offices develop programs that provide sources of auxiliary revenue.

EXPENDITURES

At the international level, primary expenditures are as follows: appropriations for divisional budgets, general operational responsibilities, evangelism initiatives, education appropriations, and appropriations set by the International General Assembly (e.g., aged ministers, disabled ministers, and ministers' widows).

Administrative costs include providing compensation for executive, administrative, and other office personnel. The basic compensation for executives and administrative leaders includes a salary set by the International Executive Council, one-half Social Security tax, minimum 5 percent of compensation for retirement plan, medical insurance, housing, and reimbursement of official ministry expenses incurred at the international level. Operational expenditures include those financial responsibilities necessary to maintain facilities and properties such as the International Offices, grounds, and other office buildings.

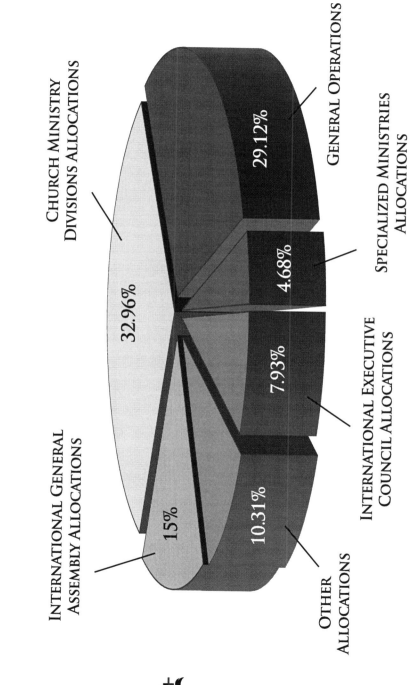

Church of God
Percentage of the Budgeted Tithe Distribution, 2012

- Church Ministry Divisions Allocations
- General Operations — 29.12%
- Specialized Ministries Allocations — 4.68%
- International Executive Council Allocations — 7.93%
- International General Assembly Allocations — 15%
- Other Allocations — 10.31%
- 32.96%

The "tithe dollar" (approved percentage of tithes from local churches) received at the International Offices is distributed in the following six major categories: (See chart, *Percentage of the Budgeted Tithe Distribution, 2012*):

- General Operations (29.12%) are disbursements for general operational responsibilities, including administrative and personnel compensation, office expense, and maintenance of facilities of the International Offices.

- Church Ministry Divisions Allocations (32.96%) are appropriations approved by the International Executive Council for administrative support of the various church ministry division budgets.

- International General Assembly Allocations (15.0%) are appropriations designated by the International General Assembly for aged ministers, disabled ministers, and ministers' widows.

- International Executive Council Allocations (7.93%) are appropriations for support of ministry needs at local, state/regional, and international levels.

- Specialized Ministries Allocations (4.68%) are disbursements approved by the International Executive Council for operational assistance of the computer center, insurance, Internet ministries, media, communications, and public relations.

- Other Allocations (10.31%) are appropriations approved by the International Executive Council for debt servicing, the convening of the International General Assembly, and designated emergency funds.

The Investment of the Missions Dollar, 2012

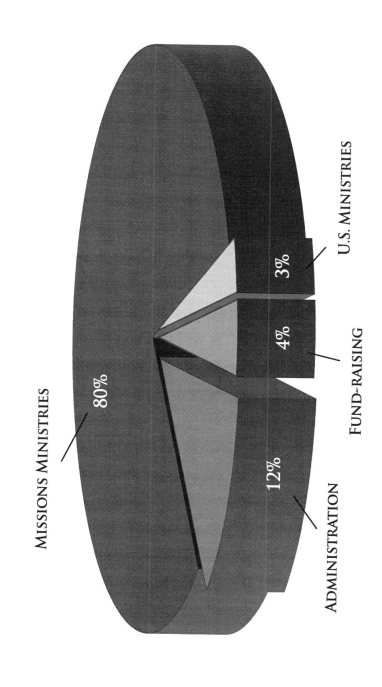

Missions Ministries 80%

Administration 12%

Fund-Raising 4%

U.S. Ministries 3%

WORLD MISSIONS GIVING

The purpose of World Missions is to support and develop an international perspective in fulfilling the mission of the church. Each local church contributes monthly an approved percentage of the tithes paid into the local treasury and forwarded to the secretary general at the International Offices. One-fourth of the approved percentage is designated for World Missions ministries.

World Missions maintains a regular program of promotion, information, and development of contributing partners. Special mission representatives of states/regions assist administrative bishops in the development and implementation of World Missions initiatives. Further, mission representatives visit local churches to share the message of missions and provide an opportunity for individuals to pledge annual support.

One hundred percent of all contributions and donations to World Missions go directly to the support of missionaries, education, church growth, and development, and missions projects. Funding for administration of the World Missions (14 percent of the total budget) comes entirely from the approved percentage of tithes received from local churches. The remaining balance of the World Missions' budget is appropriated directly to field missions ministries around the world. (See chart, *The Investment of the Missions Dollar, 2012.*)

In summary:

- Each local church contributes in missions offerings an amount equal to one-fourth of the approved percentage of tithes from local churches sent to the Cleveland, Tennessee, denominational offices. A portion of this amount supports the administration of World Missions.

- One hundred percent of contributions and donations from individuals support field missions ministries (missionaries, education, church growth, and development).

MINISTERS RETIREMENT PLAN
CHURCH OF GOD BENEFITS BOARD, INC.

The Church of God Benefits Board was incorporated to act as the trustee of the plans and funds collected through the various retirement and benefits plans maintained by the corporation. Retirement and benefits plans are provided for ministers, missionaries, evangelists, employees, and other functionaries (widows, orphans, or other beneficiaries) of the Church of God (Cleveland, Tennessee, USA) and such organizations controlled by or affiliated with the Church of God. The corporation's principal function is the administration and funding of plans and programs for the provision of retirement and welfare benefits for the ministers, missionaries, evangelists, employees, and other functionaries of the church.

For more information, contact the Benefits Board, Inc. website at *www.benefitsboard.com* or call toll free, 877.478.7190.

ACCOUNTABILITY

The Church of God financial structure provides a system of checks and balances at each level of the church. At the local level, the church treasurer, Finance Committee, and Church Council assist the pastor. In addition, each church is to submit regular reports to the congregation and monthly reports to their state or regional office. Each state or regional office is under the direct supervision of the International Executive Committee. Monthly reports are submitted to the secretary general. Ministry Divisions at the international level are responsible to the International Executive Council. Each year, an outside firm audits the financial records of the International Offices and State/Regional Offices.

All levels of the church are responsible to abide by the actions and decisions of the International General Assembly.

COMMITMENT

The administration of funds entrusted to the church by the people of God is a sacred responsibility. The magnitude of our stewardship commitment determines how we maximize ministry through the investment of tithes and offerings. The focus is not upon money. The primary focal point is upon ministry.

Stewardship is a way of life involving everything we possess. It is based upon the belief that everything we have belongs to God and that we are managers of those material blessings.

An investment is a process of committing capital (resources: economic, time, talent, energy) for an asset (ministry of the church) that is expected to produce earnings (growth and productivity) and appreciate in time (eternity). That's what it's all about. Investment in the church increases its capacity to produce. It is a factor contributing to growth both spiritually and numerically. Invest means "to endow with authority or power; to envelop with a pervasive quality; to clothe; adorn; to give; to use; and to cover completely." If the church is to fulfill its mission, it necessitates investment—investment of our calling, time, talents, and resources. When we are committed to a corporate mission, we create critical mass, and when we unite together in our investment in the Church of God, we realize spiritual dimensions beyond our capabilities. If we cease to invest in the future, the church will become plateaued and void of its vibrant spiritual dynamic.

Throughout its history, the people of the Church of God have invested of themselves sacrificially because they were focused upon a mission—a mission to fulfill their calling to share the message of Jesus Christ with the world. As a church for the twenty-first century, we can do no less. The yield is empowerment by the Holy Spirit, a harvest of souls, and a preferred future.

The greatest force for ministry in the church is you. In order to be a church for the twenty-first century, the Church of God must maintain and augment its ministry interdependence. The mutual reliance of every member, minister, and adherent of the church upon the principle of tithing and giving—*The Investment of Money*—can ensure our ability to reach the world with the message of Christ.

PART THREE

THE IMPORTANCE OF MANAGEMENT

A CALL FOR LEADERSHIP

The effectiveness, characteristics, and identity of an organization are directly related to the quality of its leadership. Leadership is at the heart of the church, both Biblically and practically. Biblically, we are called to lead; practically, we must lead. One of the greatest continuing needs in the church today is leadership development.

Ephesians 4:11, 12 states, "It was he who gave some to be apostles, some to be prophets, some to be evangelists, and some to be pastors and teachers, to prepare God's people for works of service, so that the body of Christ may be built up." God's gifts to the church are people—individuals with unique talents and abilities—who are called to do the work of ministry and build up the church. All Christians do not have the same calling; however, all have the same responsibility to use their gifts in ministry. In practical terms, some are called to be spiritual leaders and others to be followers. Everyone's gift is not leadership. Nonetheless, a good follower is as important as being a good leader. Leaders are given to the church to equip believers so that all might do the work of ministry together and strengthen the body of Christ.

In the local church, every member plays a significant and important role in the church's life. The church needs every member. Its unity is expressed through the unique and diverse gifts God gives its constituents. Regardless of the role in ministry, the calling is clear.

At each level of the church, God calls spiritual leaders. According to the Scriptural model, leadership is defined not by what one does but what one is. Some are called as pastors, some as evangelists; others are called as overseers and administrators. No matter the calling, it is a sacred task that requires the highest level of integrity and maturity. The call to ministry is a Spirit-generated compulsion to serve Christ. It is a consuming passion—a call to self-surrender, to sacrifice, to servanthood. The servant image views leadership, not as position, power, or prestige, but as service and dedication. It is a compelling call.

MANAGEMENT MODEL

An organization is a systematic arrangement of people to accomplish some specific goal or purpose. A church is an organization that has a distinct mission, includes people or members, and has a systematic structure. Management refers to the process of getting activities completed efficiently with and through people. The process represents the functions defined as planning, organizing, leading and administrating activities in order to attain specific goals (Robbins, Management, 1994).

Management functions at all levels of the church include the following:

- *Planning*—defining goals, developing strategies, and coordinating ministry activities.

- *Organizing*—determining what needs to be accomplished, who will do it, and how it will be done.

- *Leading*—directing and motivating constituents.

- *Administrating*—monitoring all ministry activities and ensuring that goals and objectives are accomplished.

The Church of God is centrally organized with administration from the local, state or region, and international levels. The church management model embraces a concentric mode of operation. Generally, Christ is at the center of the church, and all the parts connect interdependently. The same concentric approach is at the heart of management for every level of the church. On the local level, the pastor is at the center, and the various ministries are interdependently united. At the state or regional level, the administrative bishop is at the core, and all the departments are integrally connected. At the international level, the general overseer and the International Executive Committee are at the center administratively, and all the divisions and their agencies are interdependently linked.

INTERNATIONAL GENERAL ASSEMBLY

"The International General Assembly of the Church of God (Cleveland, Tennessee, USA) is that organized body with full power and authority to designate the teaching, government, principles, and practices of all the local churches composing said Assembly" (*Church of God General Assembly Minutes,* 74th A., 2012, S3, I., 1, p.65).

The International General Assembly is the highest governing body of the Church of God. It governs the operation of the Church of God at all structural levels, including international, national, state or region, district, and local. All church leaders, ministers, congregations, and members are under the jurisdiction of the International General Assembly.

When the International General Assembly convenes, it "is composed of all members and ministers of the Church of God 16 years of age and above. Members and ministers of the Church of God present and registered at the International General Assembly shall comprise its voting constituency" (74th A., 2012, S2, Article VI, 1., pp. 60-61). These members and ministers present and registered at the International General Assembly do not have a delegated relationship to their local church. However, they are representatives of all the local churches of the Church of God.

The chief purpose of the International General Assembly is to study the Scriptures and determine the Biblical position in relation to doctrine, polity, and the Christian life.

Local churches have a direct relationship with the International General Assembly even though this relationship is not bound together by authorized delegates from local churches to the Assembly. When local churches are officially "organized" and received into the Church of God, they become the constituents of the International General Assembly. All local churches accepted into the Church of God are bound by the decisions of the International General Assembly in matters of doctrine, teaching, and polity.

INTERNATIONAL GENERAL COUNCIL

The International General Council is composed of all ordained bishops of the Church of God, who comprise its voting ranks. The International General Council meets concurrently with the session of the International General Assembly. It considers and prepares recommendations in matters pertaining to the welfare of the church. The recommendations are then presented to the International General Assembly for final disposition.

In addition, the International General Council nominates to the International General Assembly the International Executive Committee (general overseer, assistants, and secretary general), general and assistant directors of Youth and Discipleship, and the director and assistant of World Missions. It also elects the members of the Council of Eighteen (elected representatives of the International Executive Council).

LOCAL STRUCTURE

The local church is the foundation and heart of all ministry activities in the Church of God. Both state/regional and international levels of the church focus their goals and objectives toward affirming, resourcing, and strengthening the ministry of the local church.

PASTOR

Management of the local church resides under the authority and responsibility of the pastor. The pastor is the principal leader of the local church. All pastors of local churches are appointed by the administrative bishop subsequent to consultation with the local congregation and an opportunity for the local church to express its pastoral preference.

The word pastor literally means "shepherd." The shepherding dimension of a pastor's responsibilities includes knowing and listening to the flock, watching out and caring for the flock, feeding and correcting the flock, and spending a great portion of time with the flock. Shepherds endear themselves to their flock.

In addition to the shepherding dimension, Scripture points to a defining leadership role in the pastor's home exemplified with spiritual maturity. These characteristics reflect the task of oversight or management. The call to pastor is a Biblical mandate to shepherd the flock, provide spiritual vision and direction, and demonstrate servant leadership.

Management and administration of the local church resides under the authority of the pastor with cooperation from the Church and Pastor's Council, the church treasurer or administrator, Finance Committee, and trustees. (See *Part Two—The Investment of Money* for discussion of church treasurer and Finance Committee). Each local church and pastor is under the supervision of the district overseer and the jurisdiction of the state or regional administrative bishop. (See chart, *Church of God Local Structure*.)

PASTORAL STAFF

Each local church may have full-time, part-time, or volunteer staff determined by need, the size of the congregation, and financial resources. The pastoral staff may include a wide variety of positions based upon the ministry areas. For example, pastoral staff may include assistant pastor(s), minister of music, minister of youth, minister of discipleship, minister of visitation, and others determined by the unique needs of the local congregation.

In churches with multiple pastoral staff members, the pastor may be designated as the lead pastor. Generally, members of the pastoral staff, regardless of position, are directly responsible to the pastor.

CHURCH AND PASTOR'S COUNCIL

When a local church considers it practical to have a Church and Pastor's Council, the governing body of the church, consisting of the loyal membership, elects the council. Members of the Church and Pastor's Council are loyal members of the church. The council is elected biennially by ballot, and a system of rotation with tenure limitations may be utilized. The pastor serves as chairman of the Church and Pastor's Council and calls all meetings.

Qualifications for Church and Pastor's Council

A member of the council must . . .

- Be a loyal member of the church, adhering to its teachings.

- Be baptized in the Holy Spirit.

- Be faithful in tithing.

- Attend church regularly.

- Work in harmony with the local, state, and general church's program and reflect a cooperative attitude toward the progress of the church.

Duties and Responsibilities

The Church and Pastor's Council, under the direction of the pastor, shall promote the general and state outreach programs of the church. The council shall work in harmony with the pastor and assist him/her, when called upon, in the institution and direction of the local church program in the following areas:

- Spiritual—encourage spiritual growth of the local congregation.

- Financial—approve the disbursement of church funds.

- Physical—provide and maintain facilities for the congregation and pastor's residence.

LOCAL BOARD OF TRUSTEES

Each local church that owns any property (either real estate or personal property) appoints a Local Board of Trustees. This board consists of not less than three members and is selected by the local congregation.

Duties and Authorities

Members of the Local Board of Trustees hold office until their successors are appointed. There is no term limitation. The trustees hold title to, manage, and control—according to the directions of the local congregation and in accordance with the *General Assembly Minutes*—all real estate and personal property owned by the local congregation by which they were selected.

The board has the full right, power, and authority for the following: to buy property for the use or benefit of the local congregation; sell, exchange, transfer, and convey any of the local property held by it, or borrow money and pledge the said property for repayment; and execute all necessary deeds.

These actions can be taken only under specific conditions that include: (1) the proposition first be presented to the local church in a conference; (2) presided over by the administrative bishop, or one whom he may appoint; (3) approved by a two-thirds majority vote; and (4) the board have approval, in writing, from the administrative bishop, or one whom he may appoint, that the proposition is not adverse to the interest of the Church of God.

CONFERENCES

Local churches transact any necessary business of the church in conferences—either regular or called. Regular conferences consist of the church membership and are convened to inform the church of its financial status and to consider any other business referred to it by the pastor and Church Council. A called conference is convened to take care of business arising between regular conferences. It consists of all members of the local church who wish to attend.

LOCAL CHURCH MINISTRIES

The greatest resource of the church is you. Each individual should be committed to ministry endeavors in the local church. Many churches maintain a wide spectrum of ministries that may include some of the following: music, youth, young adults, senior adults, singles, discipleship, Christian day schools, day care centers, education, women's ministries, men's ministries, media, visitation, witnessing, Bible studies, prayer groups, and many more.

As the Church of God continues to progress and move forward, new ministry paradigms will emerge that will require various new types of leaders, such as . . .

- Leaders who are attuned to their culture and people.

- Leaders who are relational with people in the church and community.

- Leaders who are visionary.

- Leaders who communicate well.

- Leaders who have integrity.

CHURCH OF GOD
LOCAL STRUCTURE

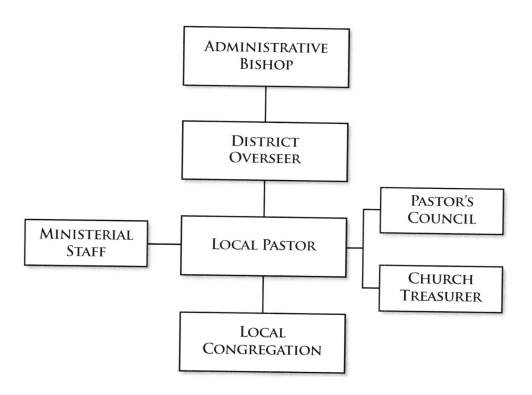

Pastors and lay leaders are partners in ministry. They provide the management functions of planning, organizing, leading, and administrating the outreach, growth, and development of the local church. The local church is God's primary force in evangelizing the world and discipling believers in the fulfillment of the Great Commission. Each local church is encouraged to follow the Scriptural pattern in identifying, training, and affirming those individuals gifted in ministry. The Church of God emphasizes the doctrinal position of the priesthood of all believers and encourages laity to assume a rightful Biblical role as full partners in ministry throughout every area of the church.

PROFILE: AVERAGE USA/CANADA CHURCH OF GOD

A statistical review for the fiscal year of 2012 provides a profile of the average local Church of God in the USA and Canada.

Membership	158
Membership by gender:	
Male	66
Female	91
Morning Worship Attendance	99
Sunday School Attendance	77

AFFILIATION WITH THE CHURCH OF GOD
—ASSOCIATE CHURCH

Non-Church of God churches that wish to affiliate with the Church of God are allowed to join as an associate church. They are able to retain ownership of their properties. However, they must show acceptance of the faith, government, polity, and practices of the Church of God, and willingness to abide by the actions of the International General Assembly as it relates to their status as an Associate Church. Associate churches must accept the basic doctrinal commitments, teachings, and practical commitments as stated in the *Book of Minutes, Church of God Book of Discipline, Church Order and Governance*.

Associate churches must submit monthly reports to the state/regional and International Offices with the same financial accountability as all International General Assembly congregations. Further, the Associate Church pastor must maintain Church of God ministerial credentials in accordance with the church's polity.

DISTRICT STRUCTURE

Each of the states or regions are divided into districts. Each district is comprised of a group of churches with boundaries determined by the administrative bishop. The purpose of districts is to assist the organization of the state program and provide oversight of the churches on the district by a district overseer. (See chart, *Church of God District Structure*.)

Each district overseer is appointed by the administrative bishop and has the following duties and responsibilities:

- Conduct conferences in local churches on the district or authorize the local pastor to conduct the conference.

- Promote a general evangelistic effort on the district each year.

- Oversee that the state program is carried out in the churches on the district.

- Assist the administrative bishop in the appointment of pastors, when called upon to do so.

- Together with the administrative bishop, pass on the selection, purchase, and construction of all church properties on the district.

CHURCH OF GOD
DISTRICT STRUCTURE

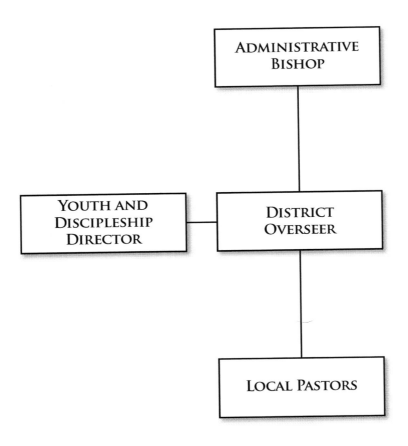

STATE OR REGIONAL STRUCTURE

The state or regional level of management is broader than the district level and holds greater authority. Each local church and pastor is under the authority and jurisdiction of the administrative bishop.

Each local church is designated as part of an individual state or regional office in the USA and Canada. State or regional offices provide established boundaries with designation of specific local churches under the jurisdiction of that office. Some states are divided into two jurisdictions because of the larger number of churches in a state (e.g., east and west, north and south). Other states are combined into regions where ministry demands and operational requirements are best accomplished (e.g., North Central, Rocky Mountain, etc.).

The management of a Church of God state or regional office is under the supervision of the administrative bishop.

ADMINISTRATIVE BISHOP (STATE OVERSEER)

The administrative bishop is the chief officer of the Church of God in each state or region. A state or regional administrative bishop can also be designated by the title of state overseer. He is appointed by the International Executive Committee at the International General Assembly and serves a two-year term of office. He may be reappointed every two years for a maximum tenure of 12 years. He is directly responsible to the International Executive Committee to organize, implement, and administer the total program and ministries of the Church of God in a given state or region. (See chart, *Church of God State Structure*.)

Qualifications
The office of administrative bishop is an honored and vital position in the Church of God. This leader must be a person of strong spiritual authority and demonstrate the following leadership qualities:

- The ability to oversee people as well as programs.

- An attitude of submission to those over him in the Lord.

- The ability to motivate and delegate responsibilities for efficient operation.

- Sensitivity to those whom he serves by exemplifying compassion, trustworthiness, concern, and integrity.

- Adaptability to the cultural differences and changing role of church ministry.

Duties and Authorities

The Administrative Bishop shall . . .

- Arrange for and assist in conducting a general evangelistic campaign throughout the state or region.

- Appoint district overseers and pastors and make changes or fill vacancies in pastorates when necessary.

- Approve the setting in order of churches before organization is effective.

- Approve the selection, purchase, and construction of all local church properties, together with the respective district overseer.

- Officiate at all ordination services in the state or region and sign credentials of all ministers in the state or region who have been approved.

- Sign the revocation form when terminating the ministry of any individual.

- Discontinue inactive churches.

- Transfer members of churches which have ceased to exist, to the church most convenient for the member.

- Appoint any officer in a local church when necessary.

- Pass on all questionnaires of applicants to the ministry in the state or region, and endorse applications before submitting to the general overseer.

- Decide the bounds of each district in the state or region.

- Report the organization of new churches to the secretary general.

- Conduct a convention on each district once each year, or group two or more districts for one convention, and at least one state convention.

- Call district or state ministers meetings or prayer conferences.

- Have the approval of the International Executive Committee before launching large financial state projects.

- Authorize exhorters to pastor churches, baptize, and receive members into the church when necessary.

- Make monthly reports to the general overseer.

- Live in the state or region over which he is overseer.

STATE COUNCIL

Each state or region has as part of its structure a State Council. The State Council serves as a group of counselors from the ministers and churches of the state or region to the administrative bishop. They are elected by the ministers of each state or region in a called conference of the ministers.

The number of churches in the state or region determines minimum size of the State Council, ranging from four to twelve members.

The State Council serves with the administrative bishop in certain governance functions at the state level. By virtue of the office, the administrative bishop serves as ex officio chairman. Members of this group must be ordained bishops where possible. They meet at the discretion of the administrative bishop and the ministers of the state or region.

Duties and Authorities
The State Council shall . . .

- With the administrative bishop, have supervision of the state missions money, surplus tithes, state parsonage, campground, and all other funds received and disbursed by the state treasury.

- After state office expenses have been paid, be authorized to use the surplus tithe of tithes from the state treasury to supplement the income of underpaid pastors and evangelists.

- Meet as often as the ministers and the administrative bishop deem necessary.

- Consider and pass on appeals and applications for help on new projects, evangelism, needy ministers, or such emergencies as may arise from time to time.

- Counsel and act with the administrative bishop in the study and preparation of recommendations for the State Ministers Conference.

- With the administrative bishop, employ the state secretary and treasurer.

STATE LEADERSHIP

Some of the states or regions have other full-time administrative positions. These may include the director of youth and discipleship and a state secretary-treasurer, other support personnel, and a state director of Women's Discipleship (normally the spouse of the administrative bishop).

Director of Youth and Discipleship

The director of youth and discipleship is nominated by the administrative bishop and elected by the State Council for a two-year term. Term limitations apply to the position with a director serving a maximum of eight consecutive years in a respective state or region. The ministers of the respective state or region elect a State Board of Youth and Discipleship. The director and board function under the supervision of the administrative bishop.

Primary responsibilities include the promotion and implementation of discipleship in the local churches. In addition, the director plans, promotes, and directs major Youth and Discipleship programs throughout the state or region. These programs include the following: youth camps, Sunday school, Family Training Hour, YWEA (Youth World Evangelism Action) youth missions fund-raising, Teen Talent, conferences, training seminars, and many others.

Director of Evangelism and Missions (USA Missions)

The director of Evangelism and Missions is nominated by the administrative bishop and elected by the State Council for a two-year term. Term limitations apply to the position with a director serving a maximum of eight consecutive years in a respective state or region.

Boards and Committees

A number of state ministry boards and committees are appointed by the administrative bishop. These boards and committees are comprised of representative ministers and laity from the respective state or region. They include the State World Missions Board, State Board of Trustees, Women's Discipleship Board, State Music Board or committee, State Ministerial Examining Boards or committees, and others as deemed necessary.

STATE MINISTRY PROGRAMS

As prescribed by the polity of the Church of God, each local church is part of a state or region. Throughout the church, there are general programs, initiatives, evangelism outreach, and resources that are common to all states or regions and local churches.

Management at the state or regional level serves to coordinate, promote, and implement general ministry programs, as well as special programs unique to the respective state or region.

Church of God
State Structure

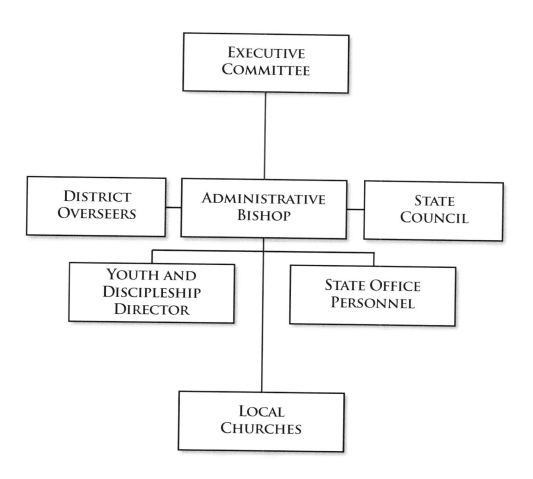

EXECUTIVE COMMITTEE

DISTRICT OVERSEERS

ADMINISTRATIVE BISHOP

STATE COUNCIL

YOUTH AND DISCIPLESHIP DIRECTOR

STATE OFFICE PERSONNEL

LOCAL CHURCHES

INTERNATIONAL STRUCTURE

The International General Assembly is the highest authority of the Church of God and governs the operation of the church at all structural levels. (See International General Assembly section.) During its scheduled meeting, the International General Assembly elects executive officers of the church, addresses matters of doctrine and polity, and provides opportunity for worship and fellowship.

INTERNATIONAL EXECUTIVE COMMITTEE

Management and leadership functions of the church at the international level are the responsibility of the International Executive Committee. The International Executive Committee is nominated by the International General Council and elected by the registered delegates to the International General Assembly for a four-year term of office, and is eligible to serve no more than eight consecutive years in this office or on the International Executive Committee. These officers include the following:

- General Overseer
- First Assistant General Overseer
- Second Assistant General Overseer
- Third Assistant General Overseer
- Secretary General

The International Executive Committee members may also be designated by the following titles while holding these specific positions:

- General Overseer—Presiding Bishop
- International Executive Committee members—Executive Bishop

Each of the five officers is assigned a specific portfolio of ministry responsibilities and also serves as the divisional director of specific ministry divisions. (See chart, *Church of God International Structure*.)

Duties and Authorities

The International Executive Committee shall . . .

- Appoint all state and provincial overseers.

- Be authorized to permit administrative bishops in mission states to continue their work, when necessary, beyond the usual tenure limitation.

- Appoint all general standing boards and committees.

- Appoint the presidents of church colleges.

- Appoint boards to hear cases of appeals of ministers.

- Act as an emergency board.

- In case of emergency, with the consent of the respective division director, be given authority to transfer money, temporarily, from one division agency to another.

- Approve the appointments of all personnel made by the standing boards and committees.

- Be empowered to counsel with ministers of any state or region through the offices of the administrative bishop and State Council with reference to any change in the state that is deemed advisable to properly carry out an effective operational program, subject to the ratification of the ministers in the respective state.

GENERAL OVERSEER (PRESIDING BISHOP)

The general overseer is the highest executive officer of the Church of God and is responsible for the general supervision of the church.

Duties and Authorities

The general overseer shall . . .

- Act as chairman or moderator of the International General Assembly, International General Council, and the International Executive Council.

- Issue and sign credentials to ministers.

- Keep a record of all the ministers within the bounds of the International General Assembly.

- Look after the general interests of the churches.

- Together with the International Executive Council, give one of the assistants the World Missions portfolio and assign duties and authorities.

- Together with the International Executive Committee, appoint all general standing boards and committees biennially.

- Together with the International Executive Committee, appoint all state and provincial overseers biennially.

- Together with the International Executive Committee, dismiss any appointee in case of necessity.

- In the event of any emergency which warrants doing so, call the Council of Eighteen and associate councilors into session for counsel.

- Call the International Executive Council or the International General Council into session.

- Approve and sign all ministry credential revocations.

ASSISTANT GENERAL OVERSEERS AND SECRETARY GENERAL

The International Executive Committee is comprised of the general overseer, three assistant general overseers, and the secretary general. Duties and authorities of the three assistant general overseers are to assist the general overseer as prescribed by the International General Assembly.

In addition to responsibilities as a member of the International Executive Committee, the secretary general is responsible for the following:

- To maintain all records and reports of the ministers and churches coming to the International Offices.

- To serve as custodian of all general church records and legal documents.

- To serve as the chief management officer of all financial matters, including receipts, disbursements, external audits, assets, and liabilities.

INTERNATIONAL EXECUTIVE COUNCIL

The International Executive Council is comprised of the International Executive Committee and 18 elected members; and, in accordance with the Memorandum of Agreement, the moderator of the Full Gospel Church of God in Southern Africa shall be a member of the International Executive Council of the Church of God in America.

Commonly, the 18 elected members are referred to as the Council of Eighteen, elected by the International General Council biennially for a two-year term. A member is eligible to succeed himself for one term. The International General Assembly requires that the elected 18 members be comprised of not less than nine pastors at the time of election and at least two members identified as foreign nationals residing and ministering outside the USA at the time of their election.

All members of the International Executive Council must be ordained bishops and no executive director, or assistant, of any church ministry who presents a budget to the International Executive Council is eligible to serve on the council.

This council considers and acts upon any and all matters pertaining to the general interest, welfare, operation and management of the Church of God. At a time set by the general overseer, the council meets and adopts recommendations to be brought before the International General Council, distributes tithes sent to the International Offices, addresses any doctrinal or polity matters for referral to the International General Assembly, and fulfills other duties prescribed by the International General Assembly.

MINISTRY DIVISIONS

All of the specific ministries of the Church of God are divided into five divisions and one additional area designated as General Ministries. International Executive Committee members serve as the divisional directors of the various divisions.

Several division ministry executives are nominated by the International General Council and elected by the International General Assembly. These positions include the following:

- Director and Assistant Director of Youth and Discipleship
- Director and Assistant Director of World Missions

All other ministry directors and assistants are appointed by the International Executive Committee. Most of the divisions operate with boards comprised of men and women, ministers and laity who provide counsel, guidance, and supervision. The International Executive Committee appoints all standing boards and committees.

Church of God Divisional Structure

(See S6. International Executive Committee, I. 4., p. 73)

General Overseer

Administrative Staff
Ministry Divisions
Prayer Commision
Church of God Foundation

Missional Resources
Communications Staff
Legal Services

Assistant General Overseer Divisional Director

Division of Care Ministries

Chaplain's Commission
Chaplains
Ministerial Care
Ministry to Israel
Ministerial Advocate
Operation Compassion
Peniel
Widows/Children
Maintenance and Security

Assistant General Overseer Divisional Director

Division of Education Ministries

Historical Commission
Ministerial Development
School of Ministry
USA Hispanic Education
International Education
Lee University
Pentecostal Theological Seminary

Assistant General Overseer Divisional Director

Division of World Evangelization

USA Missions
Amalgamations/Affiliations
Black Ministries
Church Planting
Hispanic Ministries
Editorial Evangélica
Ministry to the Military
Multi-Cultural Ministries
Haitian, Portuguese, Romanian, and Southwest Indian Ministries
Personal Evangelism
World Missions
Men/Women of Action
People for Care and Learning

Secretary General Divisional Director

Division of Discipleship Ministries

Adult Discipleship: Men
Adult Discipleship: Women
Music & Discipleship Resources
Publications Ministry
Youth and Discipleship

Support Services

Benefits Board (Consultative Only)
Business and Records
Computer Information Services
Mail Center

INTERNATIONAL EXECUTIVE COMMITTEE

GENERAL OVERSEER

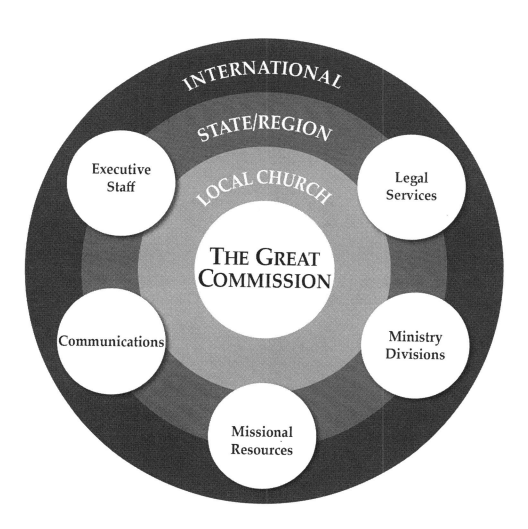

INTERNATIONAL

STATE/REGION

LOCAL CHURCH

THE GREAT COMMISSION

Executive Staff

Legal Services

Communications

Ministry Divisions

Missional Resources

ASSISTANT GENERAL OVERSEERS AND SECRETARY GENERAL

DIVISION DIRECTORS (LEADERS)

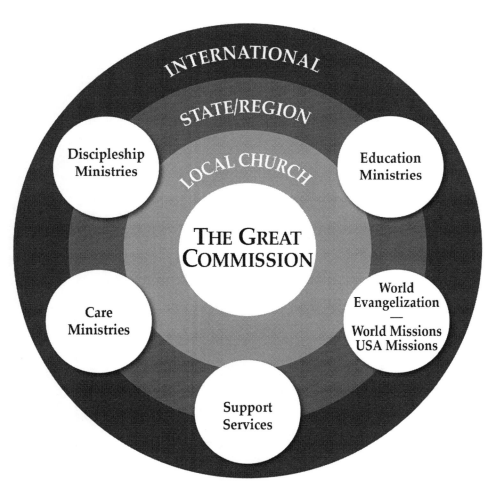

The ministry divisions and their agencies are as follows:

GENERAL MINISTRIES
- Administrative Staff to the General Overseer
- Communications Staff
- Prayer Commission
- Church of God Foundation, Inc.
- Legal Services

DIVISION OF CARE MINISTRIES
- Chaplain's Commission
- Chaplains
- Ministerial Care
- Ministry to Israel
- Ministerial Advocate
- Operation Compassion
- Peniel
- Widows/Children
- Maintenance and Security

DIVISION OF EDUCATION MINISTRIES
- Historical Commission
- Ministerial Development
- School of Ministry
- USA Hispanic Education
- International Education
- Lee University
- Pentecostal Theological Seminary

DIVISION OF WORLD EVANGELIZATION
- USA Missions
- Amalgamations/Affiliations
- Black Ministries
- Church Planting
- Hispanic Ministries *Editorial Evangélica*

- Ministry to the Military
- Multicultural Ministries
  Haitian, Portuguese, Romanian, and Southwest Indian Ministries
- Personal Evangelism
- World Missions
  Men/Women of Action, People for Care and Learning

DIVISION OF DISCIPLESHIP MINISTRIES
- Adult Discipleship: Men
- Adult Discipleship: Women
- Music and Discipleship Resources
- Publications Ministry
- Youth and Discipleship

DIVISION OF SUPPORT SERVICES
- Church of God Benefits Board, Inc. (Consultative Only)
- Business and Records
- Computer Information Services
- Mail Center

Each of the divisions maintains and provides specialized programs and resources for ministry throughout the church. The main focus of all programs is upon strengthening the local church by providing resources, materials, training, coordination, promotion, and support. Many of the divisions sponsor a wide variety of regular conferences and seminars at local, state, regional, and international levels.

Most of the divisional offices are located in Cleveland, Tennessee. The International Offices encompasses the main campus, additional off-site office buildings, and other agencies, including Lee University, Pathway Press, and the Pentecostal Theological Seminary.

WORLD MISSIONS

The Church of God vests its missions ministry in Church of God World Missions which is part of the Division of World Evangelization. World Missions is directed by an appointed board, director, and assistant director and other key personnel.

The heart of World Missions ministry is the implementation of a global strategy of evangelism, church planting, and training. To support its ministries, World Missions prepares a budget and raises funds through the efforts of their personnel and appointed missionaries. The World Missions staff performs editorial, public relations, production, financial, and administrative functions for missionaries on the field and for the constituency of North America.

A missionary, as identified by World Missions, is a person under appointment and receiving support who performs ministry in the context of geography or culture other than his/her own. World Missions selects individuals for cross-cultural ministry from various countries and also recognizes the valuable ministry of indigenous national leaders and ministers.

Missionary service on the field takes various forms, including teaching or administering in educational institutions and programs, serving in medical ministries, planting new churches, working in relief and development efforts, and many other areas. Reaching souls for Jesus Christ is at the heart of missions.

Church of God World Missions declares its commitment to the position that the local church is the indispensable key to missions success and effectiveness. Local churches produce missionaries, as well as provide financial and spiritual support. World Missions affirms its unswerving support for the development of strong local churches, strives to maintain communication with local church pastors and leaders, and urges missionaries to sustain close ties with local congregations.

WORLD MISSIONS FIELD STRUCTURE

Church of God World Missions is part of the Division of World Evangelization and operates under the supervision and authority of the International General Assembly, Executive Council, and the International Executive Committee. For administrative purposes, World Missions divides the world into several fields of ministry. These include the following:

- Africa
- Asia/Pacific
- Caribbean
- Europe/CIS/Middle East
- Latin America
- North America

The church provides structure, governance, support, and accountability for the personnel of World Missions. Internally, its lines of authority flow from the International Executive Committee to the World Missions Board and the director and assistant director of World Missions. Its field structure includes field directors and council, regional superintendent and council, national/territorial overseer and council, district overseer, and local pastors and churches. (See chart, *Church of God World Missions Field Structure.*)

INTERNATIONAL COUNCIL

The function of the International Council is to advise the International Executive Council on issues of international concern and to suggest possible items related to ministry in the international community for inclusion on the agenda of the International General Council. Its purpose is to provide greater involvement in order to support continued development of an international perspective in fulfilling the mission of the Church of God. The advisory capacity of the International Council ensures the sponsorship of ministries that meet the needs of people from different cultural settings. This forum embraces a posture that includes both participation and representation in general church functions and opportunities for leadership experience and open channels for new ideas.

The membership of the International Council is comprised of the following:

- International Executive Committee

- Director and assistant director of World Missions

- Moderator of Southern Africa

- Overseer of Indonesia

- Two members (ordained bishops), at least one being African-American and Hispanic-American appointed by the International Executive Committee

- The field director and one selected representative (ordained bishop) from each of the field areas

- Others as approved by the International Executive Council

The International Council is moderated by the general overseer and meets at least once every two years prior to and with the International Executive Council in September of the year the International General Assembly does not meet.

WORLD MISSIONS
FIELD ORGANIZATION CHART

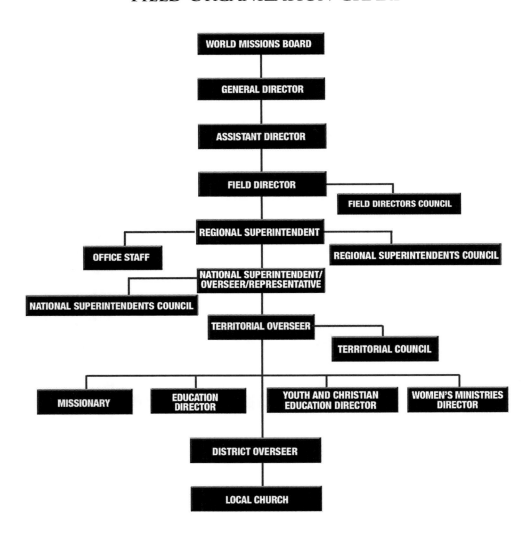

CREDENTIALED MINISTERS

One of the most important ingredients of management at every level of the church is qualified credentialed ministers. Those who have accepted the call to ministry and seek to be credentialed must complete a structured program for licensure in the Church of God.

There are five basic ranks of ministry. These include ordained bishop, ordained minister, exhorter, minister of music, and minister of Christian education. Each of these ranks requires successful completion of a ministerial internship program, practicum experience, written and oral examination, and minimum time requirements of active ministry. A lay minister's certificate may be issued to applicants who have a call of God into a specialized area of local church ministry where certification is deemed necessary and appropriate.

All credentialed ministers are to report ministerial activity to the International Offices and their state/regional office on the first of each month.

Each of these ranks is an authentic ministerial position and provides certain rights and authorities. Ordained bishop is the highest rank of ministry. Applicants for the rank of ordained bishop must meet age and active-ministry requirements, successfully complete written and oral examinations, and meet all other requirements. An ordained bishop is eligible to serve in any position or office in the Church of God.

A statistical review of the growth of churches and number of credentialed ministers during the period of 1962–2012 reveals a commitment to leadership development and church planting in the Church of God. (See chart, *Churches and Credentialed Ministers, Worldwide 1962–2012.*) During this period, new churches increased 484 percent and the number of credentialed ministers increased 450 percent.

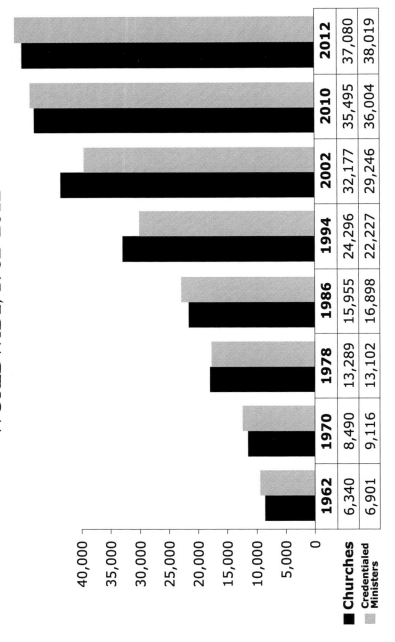

CHURCHES AND CREDENTIALED MINISTERS, WORLDWIDE, 1962–2012

	1962	1970	1978	1986	1994	2002	2010	2012
Churches	6,340	8,490	13,289	15,955	24,296	32,177	35,495	37,080
Credentialed Ministers	6,901	9,116	13,102	16,898	22,227	29,246	36,004	38,019

AFFILIATIONS

The Church of God holds membership with several nondenominational organizations, which attempt to bring together Evangelical and Pentecostal movements for interaction and fellowship. These include the following:

- National Association of Evangelicals (NAE)

- Pentecostal/Charismatic Churches of North America (PCCNA)

- Pentecostal World Fellowship (PWF)

THE IMPORTANCE OF MANAGEMENT

As an organization, the Church of God has a distinct mission that includes its greatest resource—you. Its systematic structure provides the vehicle to accomplish its goals and purpose. An essential ingredient for successful ministry is the process of management. It is only through each you of the church—called of God with unique talents, gifts for management, and leadership—that the church can fulfill its destiny.

PART FOUR

THE IMPERATIVE OF MISSION AND VISION

THE CHALLENGE

Since its beginning in 1886, the Church of God has been outstandingly blessed of God. The growth of the church is attributable to a variety of factors. Some of the more significant reasons include the following:

- Obedience to the Word of God

- Reliance upon the power and authority of the Holy Spirit

- Faithfulness to the call of Christ

- Evangelistic fervor

- Openness to all people

- World outreach

- Discipleship training

- A commitment to our heritage of Pentecostal worship, prayer, revival, and holiness.

As we face the future, it is imperative that we accept our position as one of the leading Pentecostal churches in the world. The church should view itself as a divine work of the Holy Spirit, a vital part of a spiritual movement to bring revival and renewal to a spiritually hungry world.

We live in dramatically changing times. Change is not new. It has been with us throughout history. However, today's accelerated rate of change is a new reality of seismic proportions. The lightning speed of change has altered the lives of nearly every single individual. Cultural change, economic, communication, social media, changing values, compression of time, and many other variables have changed the way we live. It is important that the church keep abreast of these modifications in order to reach a changing world for Christ. We must face change, but we should maintain commitment to spiritual values—the nonnegotiables of our walk of faith.

New churches are born as old ones die. New movements are being born into the world of change as past movements disintegrate. Historically, we have seen movements arising from dynamic moves of the Holy Spirit. From the Day of Pentecost, the Reformation, the Great Awakenings, and Evangelical revivals of recent centuries, the Pentecostal Movement, the Charismatic Renewal Movement, church growth movement, prayer movement, men's and women's movements, and others have significantly changed the shape of Protestant Christianity around the world.

While the Church of God has enjoyed tremendous growth and many congregations have been vitally involved in new spiritual movements, now is the time to examine ourselves and understand more clearly the importance of networking by sharing resources through relationships and ministry connections.

The challenge is to…

- Define direction and clarify our mission and vision.

- Set measurable goals that move us forward in the twenty-first century.

- Implement changes that effectively meet the needs of the Church of God globally.

- Invest in leadership and develop a new generation of leaders.

- Equip and mobilize the church to action.

MISSION

SIGNIFICANCE OF MISSION

The essential focus of the church should always be on its mission. While mission and vision are related, each one is uniquely distinctive. A mission statement is a brief description of an organization's fundamental purpose. It answers the question, "Why do we exist?" Mission is a general statement of what the church hopes to accomplish, whereas, vision is more specific and focuses upon strategic direction and the future. Mission can usually be described in one or two sentences and articulates the very heart of one's ministry.

CHURCH OF GOD STATEMENT OF MISSION (74th A., pp. 2012, 37-40)

The mission of the Church of God is to perpetuate the full gospel of Jesus Christ (Matthew 28:19, 20) in the Spirit and power of Pentecost (Acts 2:1-4, 6, 13-18).

The following commitments reflect the core values in regard to fulfilling the Church of God mission and vision.

PRAYER
We commit ourselves to making prayer the highest priority of the church.

PENTECOSTAL WORSHIP
We commit ourselves to gather regularly as the local expression of the Body of Christ to participate in Pentecostal worship that exalts God, engages the heart, mind, and soul, and challenges to deeper commitment and discipleship.

WORLD EVANGELIZATION
We commit ourselves to internationally reaching the unconverted, baptizing them in water, and leading them to unite with the church.

CHURCH PLANTING
We commit ourselves to identifying, training, and resourcing God-called church planters and to intentionally planting new life-giving churches.

LEADERSHIP DEVELOPMENT
We commit ourselves to identifying and developing individuals whom God has called and given leadership gifts and challenging them to become servant-leaders.

CARE
We commit ourselves to the challenge of being a church that genuinely cares for one another and for those who are lost, hurting, and needy.

INTERDEPENDENCE
We commit ourselves to the principle of interdependence, acknowledging our interconnectedness and dependence on all the members of the Body of Christ.

The goal of all we do—every program, every initiative—must be the development of growing healthy local churches. Our commitment must be to the fulfillment of the following Local Church Manifesto:

Every local church is . . .
- A worshiping community.

- An equipping community, manifesting the presence of the Holy Spirit, producing discipled, holy, growing people.

- Regularly reaching the lost for Christ.

- Engaging in world missions.

- Ministering to the poor and disenfranchised.

- Partnering with others for community impact.

- Demonstrating principles of stewardship and generosity.
  (Taken from, *Charting the Course*, R. Lamar Vest)

PRIORITY STATEMENTS

The Church of God has five major priority statements as relates to its mission. In addition, the *Church of God General Assembly Minutes* provides multiple recommendations for implementation of these key priorities (74th A., 2012, pp. 41-43).

1. **Priority Statement: LOCAL CHURCH**

    The Church of God recognizes the local church as the foundation of all ministry activities and will renew efforts to acknowledge, affirm, strengthen, and support the central importance of the ministry of the local church.

2. **Priority Statement: LAITY**

    The Church of God will further emphasize the doctrinal position of the priesthood of all believers and will encourage laity to assume a rightful Biblical role as full partners in ministry throughout every area of the church.

3. **Priority Statement: CLERGY**

    The Church of God believes that from within the priesthood of all believers, God specifically selects, calls, anoints, and commissions certain individuals for extraordinary service and leadership. This special calling (clergy) is of God's sovereign will, characterized by individuals with spiritual passion, love for the lost, total involvement, lifelong sacrifice, and servant leadership rather than by those seeking position or personal honor.

4. **Priority Statement: LEADERSHIP**

    The Church of God believes leaders must exemplify the servant qualities of Jesus (Matthew 20:27, 28; Philippians 2:17), that they must conform to the highest moral and ethical standards (Titus 1:5-9), and that they must place the welfare of others before that of themselves (John 10:11; 1 Peter 5:2).

5. **Priority Statement: CONSECRATION**
The Church of God resolutely declares that its accomplishments can never be truly reflected in numerical growth, physical accomplishments, or the adulation of men; but our true success as God's church is always measured in terms of our relationship with God through Jesus Christ.

VISION

Vision is an essential element of any effective ministry; however, it is intangible. It is defined as the experience of having perception or supernatural revelation, a mental image, something supposedly seen by other than normal sight. Spiritual vision is the ability to see God's presence, power, and plan in spite of the obstacles. It also means seeing beyond the majority—a reflection of what God wishes to accomplish through the Church of God.

Vision unifies God's people and summons increased commitment. With vision, you can read the presence and power of God into life's circumstances. It is a clear mental image of a promising future that is seen through the lens of God's eyes, seeing situations as He sees them.

Vision answers the question, *where*: *Where* do we want to go? Vision intends to serve as a clear guide to make decisions about current and future courses of action.

A philosophy of ministry is the church's core values that dictate its priorities and shape its ministry decisions. The church's strategy of ministry articulates how the church plans to accomplish its mission and vision. Strategy answers the question, *how*: *How* are we going to do what we do? The structure of ministry relates to the organization and arrangement of the various parts of the ministry, including the infrastructure that serves to fulfill the vision.

How important is it for a church to have a vision? Do we have a vision? Can we define it and verbalize it to one another? It is imperative that the Church of God answer these questions and assert a significant, focused vision for future ministry.

Why do we need a movement, a denomination, called the Church of God? The purpose of any organization is to empower ideas, inspire, equip, and mobilize its constituency around common beliefs and objectives. An organized movement, sometimes called a *denomination*, provides direction that keeps the people united, and the mission and vision alive, vibrant, and progressive.

Vision is not passive but active. It is a view of all the exciting possibilities of a preferred future. With vision, the church uses the present as a platform to launch new and needed ministry paradigms. Paul states in Philippians 3:13-14, "But one thing I do: Forgetting what is behind and straining toward what is ahead, I press on toward the goal."

An essential ingredient of vision is the belief that the mission of the church can be accomplished. Our vision should rest firmly on the bedrock of reality. While it tests the limits of what is possible, our vision remains within the realm of the feasible. Visionaries not only believe what can be, but they also are convinced that it must be, and they have a critical sense of urgency that claims their lives and pervades ministry.

Every Church of God member—every *you*—should have a vision for ministry in the twenty-first century. Without a vision of a new and more productive tomorrow, we are inclined to keep doing yesterday's status quo. If the Church of God is to continue being a cutting-edge movement, it should…

- Emphasize support and resources for local churches.

- Mobilize for world evangelization.

- Plant new life-giving churches.

- Encourage the strengthening, growth and development of all local churches.

- Utilize every communication medium available to share the gospel.

- Empower laity as effective ministry disciples.

- Enlist, equip, and train a new generation of highly competent and committed leaders.

The Great Commission remains our mandate. If the Church of God is to fulfill its vision for the future, it is essential to reaffirm its Statement of Vision. Our vision arises from our understanding of what the sovereign God purposes to do for and through His church.

CHURCH OF GOD STATEMENT OF VISION

The Church of God is to be . . .

- A movement committed to the authority of Holy Scripture for faith and direction.

- A fellowship whose worship brings God's power into the life of the church and extends that power through the lives of believers into the marketplace of life.

- A body that is directed by the Spirit, fully understanding that baptism in the Holy Spirit is both a personal blessing and an endowment of power for witness and service in fulfilling the Great Commission.

- A people who hunger for God, experience the presence of God, and stand in awe of His holiness as He changes believers into conformity with Christ.

- A New Testament church which focuses on the local congregation where the pastor nurtures and leads all members to exercise spiritual gifts in ministry.

- A church that loves all people and stands opposed to any action or policy that discriminates against any group or individual because of race, color, or nationality.

- A movement that evidences love and concern for the hurts and loneliness of the unsaved through aggressive evangelistic, discipling, and nurturing ministries.

- A church that is Christ-centered, people-oriented, and need-sensitive in all its programs and ministries.

- A movement that promotes policies and ministries which reflect an open, sincere effort to remain relevant to each generation. (*Church of God General Assembly Minutes*, 74th A., 2012, p. 37).

MINISTRY ESSENTIALS

To implement the mission and vision for ministry in the twenty-first century, the Church of God should embrace and advocate the following ministry essentials:

- *Compassion for the Unchurched*—caring enough about lost people to invest significant amounts of time, energy, and resources to reach them.

- *Great Commission Orientation*—viewing ministry potential in terms of the people still to be reached, not the limitations of facilities and/or finances, while maintaining the commitment to make disciples and multiply congregations.

- *Cultural and Generational Relevance*—utilizing a style of ministry that effectively gains a hearing with each people (ethnic representation) and generational group (children, youth, adults, and seniors).

- *Affirming and Empowering Laity*—affirming the value and importance of laity in the local church through enlistment, training, support and empowerment for ministry.

- *Discipleship Development*—accepting the responsibility to nurture believers as followers who understand commitment, comprehend the value of spiritual maturation and the empowerment of Spirit-filled believers for daily service through the practical focus of discipleship.

- *Developing, Sending, and Supporting Leaders*—recognizing that God is actively calling and commissioning leaders to multiply new churches and partnering with God by developing, sending, and supporting those leaders as they go into the harvest.

- *Pastoral Ministry*—emphasizing pastoral ministry through the identification, enlistment, training, screening, nurturing, apprenticing, and placement of the next generation of pastors.

- *Confidence in God's Sovereign Ability*—making bold plans for the future, understanding that our faith rests not in our resources but in God's sovereign ability.

- *Kingdom Perspective*—encouraging church planting by networking and partnering with like-minded members of the body of Christ to reach entire cities with the gospel.

- *Generosity*—releasing freely the people and resources needed to fulfill the Great Commission through world evangelization and the establishment of new churches.

During changing times, we should emphasize and practice the basics—our core values for ministry. These values are at the nucleus of what we do. They are always important especially during times of transition.

A COMPELLING CALL FOR CHANGE

As with other religious organizations, we now face great and complex challenges. About us are undeniable signs that tough times lie ahead for any movement attempting to survive and grow with an attitude of "business as usual." We should take an honest look at our challenges, and not complacently assume immunity to the difficulties faced by other larger, more traditional denominations—some of which are already noticeably declining.

What is the environment for change in the Church of God? Are we open, understanding, and spiritually sensitive to creativity, innovation, and new methods of ministry? Is the environment adversarial, apathetic, content with status quo, or is it supportive? The church must be responsive and supportive of a preferable future. It can be both respectful of local traditions and open to new approaches to reaching younger generations.

While many resist change, we are reminded that change in the church is normal. The entire Book of Acts chronicles church changes from the very beginning. On the Day of Pentecost, Jews became Christians and thousands were added to the church. In Acts 6, the church adopted a new form of organization to govern money when conflict arose. The church integrated its ranks in Acts 8:26-38 as Phillip witnessed to and baptized an Ethiopian and baptized him. In Acts 10, God made a major change in His dealings with mankind as He spoke to Peter through a vision; the Spirit was insistent that he should adjust his thinking and actions to this change. In Acts 11, the gospel goes to the Gentiles (change), and the house of Cornelius was filled with the Holy Spirit. In Acts 15, the entire church discussed issues at the Council in Jerusalem and accepted major change to the rules of the church. Throughout the Book of Acts and the New Testament, change is demonstrated through adaptations to different cultures, traditions, and languages. Change was a normal part of the first-century church.

The Great Commission calls for change—a change of purpose and behavior to "make disciples" and go into all the world and preach the gospel (Matthew 28:19; Mark 16:15). It is not change of doctrine and faith—these have been constant for more than twenty-one centuries—it is in the changed life that God imparts to believers. The power for fulfilling God's Great Commission is made clear in Acts 1:8: "But you will receive power when the Holy Spirit comes on you; and you will be my witnesses in Jerusalem, and in all Judea and Samaria, and to the ends of the earth." Change is a compelling call to the Pentecostal believer.

The Church of God accepts its unique position as one of the leading Pentecostal churches in the world. We are a divine work of the Holy Spirit and a vital part of a spiritual movement—a fresh revival—called to bring a renaissance of faith and renewal to a spiritually hungry world. It is a compelling call to ministry that is a Spirit-generated compulsion to serve Christ. It is a call to self-surrender, to sacrifice, and to servanthood. It is a compelling call to rethink our methods and structure and embrace effective new ministry paradigms. It is a call for the Church of God to reaffirm its mission and vision. The church should not be afraid of the "right" kind of change. Rather, it can reach forward with strategic direction and view change as a journey—a process and not an event. We are committed to fulfill the mission and vision God has given the Church of God.

STRATEGIC DIRECTION

Expectations about the twenty-first century grow more intense every day. The urgency of time calls for the Church of God to look through the lens of tomorrow, catch a glimpse of the opportunities available for ministry, and identify strategic direction for the future.

It is imperative for the Church of God to prepare for the new realities facing the church. As we envision the role of the Church of God in the future, our objective is to focus on developing ministry strategies that build on our strengths and explore the resources necessary for effective local church ministry for the generations of tomorrow. The Church of God has an unprecedented opportunity to reach beyond the status quo and fulfill our God-given mission and vision.

A ministry strategy is a process that determines exactly how we intend to accomplish our mission and vision. It answers the question "How?" and specifically states the plan of action. Strategic direction is moving from something to something. It is moving from . . .

- A comfort zone to an understanding that every nation is a mission field.

- Politically motivated leadership to a commitment of servant leadership.

- Followers of worship trends to generators of meaningful worship.

- The Sunday morning experience to a balanced ministry, including discipleship and equipping.

- The status quo to ministering with excellence.

A strategy helps to accomplish our mission, facilitates understanding, embraces positive change, enhances ministry success, provides a sense of momentum, and assists in the realization of a preferred future.

Crucial resources for implementation of our strategic directions require a commitment to a missional mentality, visionary and skilled leadership, and a positive future orientation.

MISSION AND VISION INITIATIVES

In 2012, Dr. Mark L. Williams, General Overseer, cast a vision for the Church of God arising from our understanding of what the Sovereign God purposes to do for and through His Church. The following Mission and Vision Initiatives are presented to the church directly from the heart of executive leadership and with a sense of urgency to fulfill our mission and vision.

The questions the church will face in the coming years will be . . .

- What **decisions** need to be made to position the Church of God, to effectively and faithfully fulfill its call?

- What **priorities** must be embraced to attract the hopes and dreams of a new generation of believers?

- What will it take to **implement** a push into the final frontiers of soulwinning and discipleship?

- What are the **nonnegotiables**—what are we willing to die for?

- What about **the poor, the disenfranchised, the abused**, those being sold into slavery?

- Can the Church of God reach the world?

The kind of world we live in today is drastically different from the world of past generations. Globally, the world lives under a tyranny of terror. Threats of nuclear and biological terrorism are real and frightening possibilities. The global economy has reached such a level of interdependence that a severe downturn in one country can affect economic security in another overnight. Modern business leaders are now expected to peer into the turbulent economic future and make necessary adjustments to avoid disaster for their companies. The digitalized nature of this century has created increasing expectation among people we are called upon to lead, making this unrelenting advance of communication technology both a blessing and a curse. While the Information Age has given leaders many new tools with which to lead, it has also placed heavy demands on leaders—demands previous generations of leaders never faced.

We look to many places of the world and definitely see God at work! We see Him working and moving in unprecedented ways in places like Latin America, parts of Asia, especially Indonesia and Philippines, and parts of Africa. The epicenter of Christianity is definitely moving south into the Southern Hemisphere. However, in the

undeveloped and developing countries, the Church is being perse-
cuted and is trying to survive in a hostile environment. In the de-
veloped countries, the Church finds itself increasingly marginalized
and alienated from society. North America seems to be one of the
few places in the world where the Church at large is not growing.

True to prophetic predictions—on the one hand, we see revival, we
also see an increased secularization and even apostasy. Gone are the
days of the Enlightenment. It is a world that has embraced secular
humanism, moral relativism, and denies the existence of absolute
truth. It is a world where power has shifted to those who control
information. It is a world where truth has been regulated to technology and beauty has been subjected to the eye of the beholder. It is a
world where philosophy has shifted to the existential; education has
shifted to the skeptical; the arts have shifted to the sensual; and man
has shifted to the transcendental, believing that they are their own
gods and have no need of redemption.

It is for such a time as this and into a world such as ours that you
and I have been called to lead, to stand, and to proclaim, "The Spirit
of the Lord is upon me, because He hath anointed me to preach the
gospel to the poor; he hath sent me to heal the brokenhearted, to
preach deliverance to the captives, and recovering of sight to the
blind, to set at liberty them that are bruised, to preach the acceptable
year of the Lord" (Luke 4:18,19 KJV).

Dr. Williams states:

"I do not believe for a moment that God is finished with the Church
of God. I do not believe for a moment that the best days of our movement are behind us. I believe the best is yet to come. But it will take
spiritual discernment and courage to face challenges and push forward to lay hold upon that for which Christ has laid hold upon us."

It is with that global backdrop that the executive leadership of the
Church of God vision casts five initiatives or emphases for the
Church to focus upon in the coming years. These initiatives will
not necessarily be linear in application, but rather, they will overlap
with some being concurrent. The process begins within us.

SCRIPTURES: *We want to read Scripture so that we might encounter God in a life-transforming way and take what we learn to teach others to become fully committed followers of Jesus Christ.*

The legacy of the Church of God and the stewardship of its history, values, and mission are being placed in the hands of a new generation—a generation that must rediscover the power of Scripture. The Church of God is called to begin a journey together, rediscovering the Word of God by a renewal of reading the Scripture. The executive leadership of the church is calling the entire Church of God in an initiative to R.E.A.D. the Word of God—to Reflect, Engage, Apply, and Disciple.

• **Reflect**—to read through, meditate on, and live out the Scripture.

• **Engage**—to establish a goal for 100,000 Church of God believers to read the Scriptures through each year.

• **Apply**—to live out the Word in our daily lives.

• **Disciple**—to become mature disciples modeling Christ while helping to disciple others.

SHEPHERDS: *The Church of God must give priority to affirming, resourcing, training, and caring for its shepherds.*

The men and women who serve God and the church in the pastorate are called on to carry out the mission of God in an age of religious pluralism and materialistic worldviews. This is a day when the forces of opposition seek to marginalize the church and its message. Families are being redefined. It is an age of addiction, and pastors face intense spiritual warfare almost as never before. The Church of God must give priority to affirm, resource, train, and care for its shepherds.

STUDENTS: *The burden is for a new generation of believers to rise up in the Church of God—to see our sons and daughters take their places in the body of Christ.*

The goal is to see a youth revival sweep our Church where the passion of youth intersects with the mission of God. Today, more than 40 million children in America are between the ages of 4 and 14. Around the world there are 2.3 billion children under 15 years of age. They represent the largest unreached people group in the world. The 4/14 Window must be given priority, because they are more open and receptive to the gospel than older youth and adults.

In addition, the objective of the students' initiative is to reach the Millennials—the We Generation—born between 1978 and 2000. This is the largest generation in American history. They are the first generation raised in the new postmodern world with the accompanying postmodern worldview. They are independent—politically, socially, and philosophically—they are spearheading a period of sweeping change in America and around the world. Our responsibility as a church is to reach the Millennials with the message of Christ's saving grace, so that the change they bring will be transformational change. We must ground them in a Christ-centered relational worldview, empower them in a transforming, Christlike faith, and unleash them to live out Christ's life in the world.

CITIES/CHURCH PLANTING: *The goal is to create a global plan for Urban Evangelism and Church Planting—one church, one plan and one mission.*

In light of current realities, the church must refocus on mission and vision, and recognize the opportunities to expand our missional ministry mind-set. Church planting is a Biblical blueprint for reaching the lost. We must conceive new methods of establishing new churches, discover new modes of generational engagement, intentionally create greater leadership investment, and originate a significant and relevant vision for church planting.

SOCIAL ISSUES: *The Church of God must regain its prophetic voice and speak to the social ills of our day, such as abortion, pornography, human trafficking, and the sexual exploitation of children.*

While we often are insulated from the harsh reality of the sexual exploitation that exists outside the protecting walls of our churches, consider these shocking statistics: some 300,000 children in the United States are at risk every year for commercial sexual exploitation, and some 600,000–800,000 people are bought and sold across international borders each year. Human trafficking and sexual slavery have created bondage for many children who have been kidnapped, abandoned, and raised without hope.

The responsibility for change lies with us. The process must begin within us not to close our minds prematurely to the shock of new ideas and the surprise of radical redesign. This means leading through the turbulence and resisting the idea-assassins who seem always to rush forward to suppress any new suggestion on grounds of its impracticality, while trying to manipulate the future by defending whatever now exists as practical, no matter how oppressive, no matter how archaic, no matter how dysfunctional.

It means actually beginning a process of meaningful reconstruction now—while the opportunity is great; while the need is so urgent; and while the window is still open.
(Taken from, *Message from General Overseer,* Mark L. Williams)

THE IMPERATIVE

It's hard to imagine that more than 12 decades of time have passed in the Church of God. However, we are now firmly planted into the future. At the end of the first millennium of the Christian church, approximately 275 million people lived on the earth. Today, the population of earth exceeds 6.9 billion. The opportunity for church growth and ministry is exponential. There are more than 600 million Pentecostals around the world. On the Day of Pentecost, 3,000 responded to Peter's brief message and call for believers.

From its inception, the Church of God has had its own identifying characteristics. It was organized to maintain Biblical integrity. In the midst of a world of secularism, we need to guard against compromise and focus upon the imperative of our mission and vision:

- To perpetuate the "good news" of Jesus Christ and "go into all the world and preach the gospel to every creature" (Mark 16:15 NKJV).

- To renew our pledge to do whatever is necessary to be God's people on this earth.

- To reaffirm our belief that the church is Christ-centered, people-oriented, and need-sensitive.

- To focus on the local church and the resources necessary to fulfill its ministries.

- To recognize the power and authority of the Holy Spirit in the life of the church and believers.

- To emphasize the importance of leadership development and the utilization of ministry resources.

Now is the time! The Church of God must seize the moment—the opportunity, the imperative of our mission and vision. How can this be done? It can become a reality only through the strength of the church's greatest resource—*you*. Each *you* identified, committed, equipped, nurtured, and placed into ministry.

Where is God leading the Church of God? He is directing the church as a global movement prepared to meet the demands and challenges of ministry in the twenty-first century. The church must be a driving force of Pentecost united with one accord. What will it take? It will take *YOU* and your church—together!

APPENDIX A

DOCTRINAL COMMITMENTS (74th A., 2012, pp. 23-24)

1. **Repentance.**
   Mark 1:15; Luke 13:3; Acts 3:19.

2. **Justification.**
   Romans 5:1; Titus 3:7.

3. **Regeneration.**
   Titus 3:5.

4. **New birth.**
   John 3:3; 1 Peter 1:23; 1 John 3:9.

5. **Sanctification subsequent to Justification.**
   Romans 5:2; 1 Corinthians 1:30; 1 Thessalonians 4:3; Hebrews 13:12.

6. **Holiness.**
   Luke 1:75; 1 Thessalonians 4:7; Hebrews 12:14.

7. **Water baptism.**
   Matthew 28:19; Mark 1:9, 10; John 3:22, 23; Acts 8:36, 38.

8. **Baptism with the Holy Ghost subsequent to cleansing; the enduement of power for service.**
   Matthew 3:11; Luke 24:49, 53; Acts 1:4-8.

9. **The speaking in tongues as the Spirit gives utterance as the initial evidence of the baptism of the Holy Ghost.**
   John 15:26; Acts 2:4; 10:44-46; 19:1-7.

10. **The Church.**
    Exodus 19:5, 6; Psalm 22:22; Matthew 16:13-19; 28:19, 20; Acts 1:8; 2:42-47; 7:38; 20:28; Romans 8:14-17; 1 Corinthians 3:16, 17; 12:12-31; 2 Corinthians 6:16-18; Ephesians 2:19-22; 3:9, 21; Philippians 3:10; Hebrews 2:12; 1 Peter 2:9; 1 John 1:6, 7; Revelation 21:2, 9; 22:17.

11. **Spiritual gifts.**
    1 Corinthians 12:1, 7, 10, 28, 31; 14:1.

12. **Signs following believers.**
    Mark 16:17-20; Romans 15:18, 19; Hebrews 2:4.

13. **Fruit of the Spirit.**
    Romans 6:22; Galatians 5:22, 23; Ephesians 5:9; Philippians 1:11.

14. **Divine healing provided for all in the Atonement.**
    Psalm 103:3; Isaiah 53:4, 5; Matthew 8:17; James 5:14-16;
    1 Peter 2:24.

15. **The Lord's Supper.**
    Luke 22:17-20; 1 Corinthians 11:23-26.

16. **Washing the saints' feet.**
    John 13:4-17; 1 Timothy 5:9, 10.

17. **Tithing and giving.**
    Genesis 14:18-20; 28:20-22; Malachi 3:10; Luke 11:42;
    1 Corinthians 9:6-9; 16:2; Hebrews 7:1-21.

18. **Restitution where possible.**
    Matthew 3:8; Luke 19:8, 9.

19. **Premillennial second coming of Jesus.**
    **First, to resurrect the dead saints and to catch away the
    living saints to Him in the air**.
    1 Corinthians 15:52; 1 Thessalonians 4:15-17; 2 Thessalonians 2:1.
    Second, to reign on the earth a thousand years.
    Zechariah 14:4; 1 Thessalonians 4:14; 2 Thessalonians 1:7-10;
    Jude 14, 15; Revelation 5:10; 19:11-21; 20:4-6.

20. **Resurrection.**
    John 5:28, 29; Acts 24:15; Revelation 20:5, 6.

21. **Eternal life for the righteous.**
    Matthew 25:46; Luke 18:30; John 10:28; Romans 6:22; 1 John
    5:11-13.

22. **Eternal punishment for the wicked. No liberation nor
    annihilation.**
    Matthew 25:41-46; Mark 3:29; 2 Thessalonians 1:8, 9;
    Revelation 20:10-15; 21:8.

APPENDIX B

PRACTICAL COMMITMENTS (74 A., 2012, 24-32)

I. SPIRITUAL EXAMPLE

We will demonstrate our commitment to Christ through our practice of the spiritual disciplines; we will demonstrate our commitment to the body of Christ through our loyalty to God and commitment to His church; and we will demonstrate our commitment to the work of Christ through our being good stewards.

A. Practice of Spiritual Disciplines

Spiritual disciplines involve such practices as prayer, praise, worship, confession, fasting, meditation, and study. Through prayer we express our trust in Jehovah God, the giver of all good things, and acknowledge our dependence on Him for our needs and for the needs of others (Matthew 6:5-15; Luke 11:1-13; James 5:13-18). Through both private and public worship we bless God, have communion with Him, and are provided daily with spiritual enrichment and growth in grace. Through periods of fasting we draw close to God, meditate on the passion of Christ, and discipline ourselves to submit to the control of the Holy Spirit in all areas of our life (Matthew 6:16-18; 9:14-17; Acts 14:23). Through confession of our sins to God we are assured of divine forgiveness (1 John 1:9–2:2). The sharing of our confession with other believers provides the opportunity to request prayer and to bear one another's burdens (Galatians 6:2; James 5:16). Through meditation on and study of the Word of God we enhance our own spiritual growth and prepare ourselves to help guide and instruct others in scriptural truths (Joshua 1:8; Psalm 1:2; 2 Timothy 2:15, 23-26).

B. Loyalty to God and Commitment to the Church

The life of Christian discipleship calls for the fulfillment of our duties to the body of Christ. We are to unite regularly with other members of the church for the purpose of magnifying and praising God and hearing His Word (Matthew 18:20; John 4:23; Acts 2:42, 46, 47; 12:24; Hebrews 10:25). Sunday is the Christian day of worship. As the Lord's Day, it commemorates the resurrection of Christ from the dead (Matthew 28:1) and should be employed for worship, fellowship, Christian service, teaching, evangelism, and proclamation (Acts 20:7; Romans 14:5, 6; 1 Corinthians 16:2; Colossians 2:16, 17). We are to provide for the financial needs of the church by the giving of tithes (Malachi 3:10; Matthew 23:23) and offerings (1 Corinthians 16:2; 2 Corinthians 8:1-24; 9:1-15). It is our duty to respect and to submit to those whom the Lord Jesus has placed over us in the church (1 Thessalonians 5:12, 13; Hebrews 13:7, 17). Our exercise of authority must be as a spiritual example rather than as a lord over God's flock (Matthew 20:25-28; 1 Peter 5:1-3). Furthermore, our submission must be a manifestation of the spiritual grace of humility (Ephesians 5:21; 1 Peter 5:5, 6). Finally, we are to avoid affiliation with oath-bound societies. Such societies may appear to have spiritual character, but by being oath-bound and secretive, they contradict Christian spirituality (John 18:20; 2 Corinthians 6:14-18). Christians must not belong to any body or society that requires or practices an allegiance that supersedes or excludes their fellowship in Christ (Matthew 12:47-49; John 17:21-23).

C. Being Good Stewards

In the Scriptures, the virtues of thrift and simplicity are honored, but the vices of waste and ostentation are solemnly prohibited (Isaiah 55:2; Matthew 6:19-23). The living of a godly and sober life requires the wise and frugal use of our temporal blessings, including time, talent, and money. As good stewards we are to make the most of our time, whether for recreation or for work (Ephesians 5:16; Colossians 4:5). The idle use of leisure time degrades (2 Thessalonians 3:6-13; 1 Timothy 5:13), but the edifying use of it brings inner renewal. All our work and play should honor the name of God (1 Corinthians 10:31). As good stewards we must use fully our spiritual gifts (Romans 12:3-8; 1 Corinthians 12:1-11, 27-31; Ephesians 4:11-16; 1 Peter 4:9-11) and natural talents (Matthew 25:14-30) for the glory of God. As good stewards we must recognize that the wise use of money is an essential part of the Christian's economy of life. God has committed temporal blessings to our trust (Matthew 7:11, James 1:17).

II. MORAL PURITY

We will engage in those activities which glorify God in our body and which avoid the fulfillment of the lust of the flesh. We will read, watch and listen to those things which are of positive benefit to our spiritual well-being.

A. Glorifying God in Our Body

Our body is the temple of the Holy Ghost, and we are to glorify God in our body (Romans 12:1, 2; 1 Corinthians 6:19, 20; 10:31). We are to walk in the Spirit and not fulfill the lust of the flesh (Galatians 5:16). Examples of fleshly behavior which do not glorify God are noted in several passages of Scripture (Romans 1:24; 1 Corinthians 6:9, 10; Galatians 5:19-21; Revelation 21:8). Sinful practices which are made prominent and condemned in these scriptures include homosexuality, adultery, worldly attitudes (such as hatred, envy, jealousy), corrupt communication (such as gossip, angry outbursts, filthy words), stealing, murder, drunkenness, and witchcraft. Witchcraft has to do with the practices of the occult, which are forbidden by God and lead to the worship of Satan.

B. Reading, Watching, and Listening

The literature we read, the programs we watch, and the music we listen to profoundly affect the way we feel, think, and behave. It is imperative, then, that the Christian read, watch, and listen to those things which inspire, instruct and challenge to a higher plane of living. Therefore, literature, programs, and music which are worldly in content or pornographic in nature must be avoided. A Christian is not to attend (or watch on television) movies or theatrical performances of a demoralizing nature (Romans 13:14; Philippians 4:8).

C. Benefiting Spiritual Well-Being

The use of leisure time in the life of a Christian should be characterized by those activities which edify both the individual and the body of Christ (Romans 6:13; 1 Corinthians 10:31, 32). We are to avoid places and practices which are of this world. Consequently, a Christian must not be a part of any other types of entertainment which appeal to the fleshly nature and/or bring discredit to the Christian testimony (2 Corinthians 6:17; 1 Thessalonians 5:21, 22; 1 John 2:15-17).

III. PERSONAL INTEGRITY

We will live in a manner that inspires trust and confidence, bearing the fruit of the Spirit, and seeking to manifest the character of Christ in all our behavior.

A. Trust and Confidence

A Christian should be trustworthy, dependable, and a person of his word (Matthew 5:37; 1 Peter 2:11, 12). Therefore, the swearing of oaths is contrary to a Christian's trustworthiness and should be avoided (Matthew 5:34-37; James 5:12). Christ, by precept and example, taught that we love our enemy and prefer our brother (Matthew 5:43-48; Romans 12:10; Philippians 2:3; 1 John 3:16). We should behave in a way that will point others to Christ (Matthew 5:16; 1 Corinthians 11:1).

B. Fruit of the Spirit

If we live in the Spirit, we will manifest the fruit (attitudes and actions) of the Spirit and will not fulfill the lusts of the flesh (Galatians 5:16, 22-25; 1 John 1:7). Trustful relationships with others are a natural outgrowth of our positive relationship with the Lord (Psalm 1:1-3; Matthew 22:37-40). A lack of fruit-bearing in our lives will be judged (Matthew 7:16-20; Luke 13:6-9; John 15:1-8).

C. Character of Christ

Love for others is the hallmark of the Christ-life (John 13:34, 35; 15:9-13; 1 John 4:7-11). In His relationship with His Father, Jesus displayed submission (Luke 22:42; John 4:34; 5:30). In His relationship with others, He demonstrated acceptance (John 8:11), compassion (Matthew 9:36; Mark 6:34) and forgiveness (Matthew 9:2; Luke 5:20). We cannot bear the fruit of the Spirit and manifest the character of Christ without being spiritually joined to Christ (John 15:4, 5) and without having the seed of the Word planted in our heart (John 15:3; 1 Peter 1:22, 23).

IV. FAMILY RESPONSIBILITY

We will give priority to fulfilling family responsibilities, to preserving the sanctity of marriage, and to maintaining divine order in the home.

A. Priority of the Family

The family is the basic unit of human relationship and as such is foundational to both society and the church (Genesis 2:18-24). The divine origin of the family, along with its foundational character, makes it imperative that we give priority to ministry to the family, both from a personal and corporate standpoint. The practice of Christian disciplines and virtues should begin in the home (Deuteronomy 6:6, 7). Therefore, our families should establish some pattern for family devotions and should endeavor to provide a Christian environment in the home (1 Timothy 3:3, 4; 5:8).

B. Sanctity of Marriage

Marriage is ordained of God and is a spiritual union in which a man and a woman are joined by God to live together as one (Genesis 2:24; Mark 10:7). Because of the divine character of marriage, it is a lifelong commitment with the only clear Biblical allowance for divorce being fornication (Matthew 5:32; 19:9).

Sexual involvement, either before marriage or with someone other than the marriage partner, is strictly forbidden in Scripture (Exodus 20:14; 1 Corinthians 6:15-18). Understanding the sanctity of marriage, partners should strive to maintain a happy, harmonious, and holy relationship. Should divorce occur, the church should be quick to provide love, understanding, and counsel to those involved. The remarriage of divorced persons should be undertaken only after a thorough understanding of and submission to the Scriptural instructions concerning this issue (Matthew 19:7-9; Mark 10:2-12; Luke 16:18; Romans 7:2, 3; 1 Corinthians 7:2, 10, 11). Should a Christian desire to remain single, this decision should be respected and should be seen as a viable Scriptural alternative (1 Corinthians 7:8, 32-34).

C. Divine Order in the Home

When God created man, He created them male and female (Genesis 1:27). He gave them distinctly different characteristics (1 Corinthians 11:14, 15;

1 Peter 3:7) as well as different responsibilities (Genesis 3:16-19; 1 Peter 3:1-7). In God's order, the husband is head of the home (Ephesians 5:22-31; Colossians 3:18, 19), parents are to nurture and admonish their children (Ephesians 6:4; Colossians 3:21), and children are to obey and honor their parents (Exodus 20:12; Ephesians 6:1-3; Colossians 3:20). In order for harmony to exist in the home, God's order of responsibility must be observed.

V. BEHAVIORAL TEMPERANCE
We will practice temperance in behavior and will abstain from activities and attitudes which are offensive to our fellowman or which lead to addiction or enslavement.

A. Temperance
One of the cardinal Christian virtues is temperance or self-control (1 Corinthians 9:25; Titus 1:8, 2:2). It is listed as fruit of the Spirit (Galatians 5:23). We are admonished to practice moderation and balance in our behavior (Philippians 4:5). The Scripture indicates that it is within our prerogative to control our thinking (Philippians 4:8), our anger (Ephesians 4:26), and our communication (Ephesians 4:29; Colossians 3:8). To exercise self-discipline reflects the power of God in our life (1 Corinthians 9:27; 2 Peter 1:5-11).

B. Offensive Behavior
The Bible speaks clearly that we are to be sensitive to the needs and feelings of others as a demonstration of our love for them (Matthew 22:39; Romans 12:9-21; 13:10; Philippians 2:3-5). At times it is necessary for us to control our behavior so as not to bring offense to others (Romans 14:13-21; 1 Corinthians 8:9-13). As we know Christ after the Spirit, we are also to know others in the same manner so we will not judge them after their outward behavior alone (2 Corinthians 5:16). A respect and tolerance for differences in others should characterize our relationships (Romans 14:2, 3; 1 Corinthians 8:8; Ephesians 4:2; Colossians 3:13; 1 Timothy 4:1-5).

C. Addiction and Enslavement

One of the primary benefits of our liberty in Christ is freedom from the domination of negative forces (John 8:32, 36; Romans 6:14; 8:2). We are counseled not to put ourselves again under bondage (Galatians 5:1). Therefore, a Christian must totally abstain from all alcoholic beverages and other habit-forming and mood-altering chemical substances and refrain from the use of tobacco in any form, marijuana and all other addictive substances, and further, must refrain from any activity (such as gambling or gluttony) which defiles the body as the temple of God or which dominates and enslaves the spirit that has been made free in Christ (Proverbs 20:1; 23:20-35; Isaiah 28:7; 1 Corinthians 3:17; 5:11; 6:10; 2 Corinthians 7:1; James 1:21).

VI. MODEST APPEARANCE

We will demonstrate the Scriptural principle of modesty by appearing and dressing in a manner that will enhance our Christian testimony and will avoid pride, elaborateness or sensuality.

A. Modesty

According to the Biblical idea, modesty is an inner spiritual grace that recoils from anything unseemly and impure, is chaste in thought and conduct, and is free of crudeness and indecency in dress and behavior (Ephesians 4:25, 29, 31; 5:1-8; 1 Timothy 2:9, 10). Therefore, modesty includes our appearance, dress, speech, and conduct and can be applied to all situations. The essential issue is, does our style of life please or displease God?

B. Appearance and Dress

Our life, character, and self-image are reflected by our apparel and mode of dress. The admonition of Scripture, "Be not conformed to this world," reminds us that our manner of dress must be modest and decent (Romans 12:2; 1 Thessalonians 5:22, 23). It is not displeasing to God for us to dress well and be well groomed. However, above all we must seek spiritual beauty, which does not come from outward adornment with jewelry, expensive clothes, or cosmetics, but from good works, chaste conversation, and a meek and quiet spirit (Philippians 4:8; 1 Peter 3:3-5).

C. Pride, Elaborateness, Sensuality

As godly people we are to abstain from all lusts of the flesh and avoid dressing in a manner that encourages immoral thoughts, attitudes, and life-styles (Galatians 5:13-21; 1 Peter 2:11; 2 Peter 1:4). Our beauty does not depend on elaborate, showy dress; extravagant, costly attire; or on the use of jewelry or cosmetics but on our relationship with Christ. External adorn-ment, whether clothing or jewelry, as an outward display of personal worth, is contrary to a spiritual attitude (James 2:1-4).

VII. SOCIAL OBLIGATION

It should be our objective to fulfill our obligations to society by being good citizens, by correcting social injustices, and by protecting the sanctity of life.

A. Being Good Citizens

As Christians we are members of the kingdom of God as well as a social order of this world. Obedience to God requires us to act in a responsible manner as citizens of our country (Mark 12:13-17; Romans 13:1-7; 1 Peter 2:13-17). Therefore, we should support civil law and order; hold our leaders in respect and pray for them; participate in school, community, and govern-mental activities; exercise our voting rights; and speak out on clear-cut mor-al issues. God's law is supreme, but we are to obey the laws of our country insofar as they are not in conflict with obedience to God (Acts 5:29). When it becomes necessary to disagree with practices and requirements of govern-ment, we should do so out of a concern for the promotion of righteousness and not out of delight in discord and controversy.

B. Correcting Social Injustice

Love for others and the recognition of the equal worth of all people in the sight of God (Acts 10:34; 17:26) should compel us to take steps to improve the situation of those who are underprivileged, neglected, hungry, home-less, and victimized by prejudice, persecution, and oppression (Matthew 22:39; Romans 13:8-10; 1 John 3:17). In all of our dealings, we must be sensitive to human needs (Luke 10:30-37; James 1:17) and guard against racial and economic discrimination. Every person should have freedom to worship and participate in the life of the church regardless of race, color, sex, social class, or nationality.

C. Protecting the Sanctity of Life

God alone confers life (Genesis 1:1-31); therefore, we are responsible to God to care for our physical life and that of others. If the circumstances require, we must be prepared to risk our life in the service of our neighbor (John 15:13); but the general rule is that we must respect our physical life and employ every worthy means to maintain it. Since God alone confers life, God alone must decide when it is to be ended (Psalm 31:14, 15). Because a human fetus is sacred and blessed of God, we believe that we have the responsibility to protect the life of the unborn (Jeremiah 1:5; Luke 1:41). It is our firm conviction that abortion, euthanasia of aged, mentally incompetent, terminally ill, and otherwise handicapped, for reasons of personal convenience, social adjustment, or economic advantage, are morally wrong.

Furthermore, we believe it is our Christian responsibility to care for the earth and its resources. In the beginning God gave man dominion over the earth (Genesis 1:26-30). This does not, however, give us license to pollute our natural environment or to waste the resources of the earth.

INDEX

A

administrative bishop 5, 43, 44, 47, 48,
    49, 50, 62, 64, 65, 67, 71, 73, 76,
    77, 78, 81
Assistant General Overseer 80

B

Baker, Michael L. 7, 9
Benefits Board 57, 90, 133
Benevolence 30, 52
Bluebelles 32

C

Chaplains Commission 30
Charismatic 20, 97, 100
Christian Union 15
Church and Pastor's Council 43, 65, 66
church planting 49, 91, 95, 108, 115
church treasurer 41, 42, 43, 44, 57, 65
Conferences—regular; called 7, 20, 42,
    44, 68, 71, 75, 77, 90
Covenant of Membership 25

D

Declaration of Faith 22
district 48, 63, 65, 71, 73, 74, 75, 92
Division of Care Ministries 30, 89
Division of Discipleship 37
Division of Education 31, 89
Division of Support Services 90
Division of World Evangelization 91, 92
Doctrinal Commitments 6, 24

E

Evangelical 19, 97, 100
Evangelism and Missions 77
exhorter 22, 95
expenditures 39, 44, 45, 48, 49, 50, 52

F

Finance Committee 43, 57, 65
financial system 7, 39, 40, 48
foundational 19, 125

G

General Board of Trustees 51
general overseer 48, 50, 51, 63, 64, 75,
    81, 82, 83, 84, 93
global movement 7, 15, 117
Great Commission 14, 17, 20, 70, 106,
    107, 108, 109, 110

H

Home for Children 30

I

Institutional Chaplains 30
International Executive Committee 47,
    48, 49, 50, 51, 57, 63, 64, 73, 75,
    80, 81, 82, 83, 84, 92, 93
International Executive Council 45, 50,
    51, 52, 54, 57, 64, 82, 83, 84, 92,
    93
International General Assembly 5, 21,
    24, 40, 41, 44, 46, 50, 51, 52, 54,
    57, 63, 64, 70, 71, 73, 80, 83, 84,
    92, 93
International General Council 64, 80, 82,
    83, 84, 92
International Offices 16, 44, 45, 50, 51,
    52, 54, 56, 57, 71, 83, 84, 90, 95,
    133
International Structure 5, 80

J

Joy Belles 32

L

laity 21, 22, 49, 70, 78, 84, 103, 106, 107
Lay Coordinators 32

LifeBuilders 32
Local Board of Trustees 67
local church 10, 14, 17, 21, 22, 40, 41,
    42, 43, 44, 45, 46, 47, 49, 50, 52,
    56, 61, 63, 64, 65, 66, 67, 68, 70,
    73, 75, 78, 90, 91, 95, 102, 103,
    107, 110, 117

M

membership 7, 9, 16, 25, 26, 27, 29, 37,
    38, 40, 44, 49, 66, 68, 93, 97
membership survey 27
Men's Discipleship 10, 32, 134
Men/Women of Action 90
ministers 13, 16, 17, 21, 41, 48, 52, 54,
    57, 63, 74, 75, 76, 77, 78, 81, 82,
    83, 84, 91, 95
Ministers Retirement Plan 57
Ministries 31, 32, 52, 54, 77, 78, 89, 90
Ministry to the Military 31, 90
mission 7, 15, 16, 21, 56, 58, 62, 81, 92,
    97, 100, 101, 103, 104, 105, 107,
    110, 111, 114, 115, 116, 117
missionaries 56, 57, 91
Music and Discipleship 90

N

National Association of Evangelicals 19,
    97

O

Operation Compassion 89
ordained bishop 22, 95
ordained minister 22, 95

P

pastor 9, 25, 26, 38, 41, 42, 43, 44, 45,
    57, 62, 64, 65, 66, 67, 68, 71, 73,
    75, 106
Pentecostal 7, 15, 16, 17, 20, 89, 90, 97,
    99, 100, 101, 110, 133
Pentecostal/Charismatic Churches of
    North America 97

Pentecostal World Fellowship 97
Practical Commitments 6, 24
Presiding Bishop 80

R

reports 42, 43, 44, 48, 50, 57, 71, 75, 83

S

School of Ministry 89
secretary general 42, 43, 45, 50, 52, 56,
    57, 64, 75, 83
Servicemen's Centers 31
State Board of Trustees 49, 78
State Council 48, 76, 77
statement of mission 101
statement of vision 106
state overseer 47, 73
stewardship 39, 47, 58, 102, 114
Sunday school 41, 77
Sweethearts 32

T

tithe of tithe 44, 45, 49, 50
tithe(s) 39, 40, 41, 44, 45, 46, 48, 49, 50,
    51, 54, 76

V

Vest, R. Lamar 16, 102
vision 7, 65, 100, 101, 104, 105, 106,
    107, 109, 110, 111, 113, 115, 116,
    117

W

widows care center 30
Williams, Mark L. 9, 111, 116
Women's Discipleship 32, 134
World Missions 29, 32, 50, 52, 56, 64,
    78, 82, 84, 90, 91, 92, 93

Y

Youth and Discipleship 32, 64, 77, 84, 90

CONTACTS

Church of God International Offices
P.O. Box 2430
Cleveland, TN 37320
423-472-3361
www.churchofgod.org
info@churchofgod.org

Adult Discipleship
P.O. Box 2430
Cleveland, TN 37320
423-478-7286
423-478-7170
www.coglifebuilders.com
www.womenofpowercog.org
adultdiscipleship@churchofgod.org

Lee University
P.O. Box 3450
Cleveland, TN 37311
423-614-8000
www.leeuniversity.edu
admissions@leeuniversity.edu

Pentecostal Theological Seminary
P.O. Box 3330
Cleveland, TN 37320
423-478-1131
www.ptseminary.edu
info@ptseminary.edu

Benefits Board
P.O. Box 4608
Cleveland, TN 37320
423-478-7131
www.benefitsboard.com
info@benefitsboard.com

To order *You and Your Church* Resources please contact:

Pathway Press
P.O. Box 2250
Cleveland, TN 37320
423-476-4512
www.pathwaypress.org
info@pathwaypress.org

Men's Discipleship
P.O. Box 2430
Cleveland, TN 37320
423-478-7286
www.coglifebuilders.com
mensdiscipleship@churchofgod.org

Women's Discipleship
P.O. Box 2430
Cleveland, TN 37320
423-478-7170
www.womenofpowercog.org
womensdiscipleship@churchofgod.org

YOU AND YOUR CHURCH

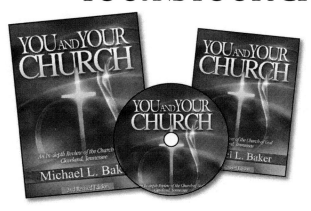

Instructor's Guide
ISBN: 978-1-59684-780-4

Introductory Booklet
ISBN: 978-1-59684-779-8

DVD
Item#: 7675 DVD